DAY TOURS FROM DUBLIN

183

By the same author

WALKS GUIDES:
The Wicklow Way
Ireland's Long Distance Walks
Ireland's Waymarked Trails
Irish Waterside Walks
Ordnance Survey Guide to the Wicklow Way
Ordnance Survey Guide to the Western Way
Ordnance Survey Guide to the Beara Way
Waterford Walks

TRAVELOGUES:
By Cliff and Shore
By Swerve of Shore
Walking across Ireland

ANTHOLOGY:
A Walk in Ireland

ARCHITECTURAL HISTORY:
The New Neighbourhood of Dublin

Day Tours
FROM
Dublin

MICHAEL FEWER

GILL & MACMILLAN

Gill & Macmillan Ltd
Hume Avenue, Park West, Dublin 12
with associated companies throughout the world
www.gillmacmillan.ie
© Michael Fewer 2006
ISBN-13: 978 07171 3820 3
ISBN-10: 0 7171 3820 8
Maps and illustrations by Michael Fewer
Design and print origination by O'K Graphic Design, Dublin
Printed by ColourBooks Ltd, Dublin

This book is typeset in 10/14 pt Adobe Caslon.

The paper used in this book comes from the wood pulp of managed forests. For every tree felled, at least one tree is planted, thereby renewing natural resources.

A CIP catalogue record for this book is available from the British Library.

The maps in this book are based on Ordnance Survey Ireland
by permission of the Government (Permit No. 8168)
© Government of Ireland

1 3 5 4 2

For Finn and Diarmuid

CONTENTS

INTRODUCTION

Located on a fine seacoast with a mountain range to the south, the Bog of Allen and the pastures of Meath to the west, and the wealthy lands of Fingal to the north, Dublin City enjoys considerable diversity and beauty in its surrounds. *Day Tours from Dublin* seeks out the best of the wealth of picturesque, entertaining, historic and even bizarre destinations within easy reach of the city, and suggests scenic routes to and from them, providing information on good places to picnic, take refreshments, lunch, or an evening meal before completing the tour.

There are attractions to appeal to everyone in the family. The more out-of-the-way, overgrown castles, old churches and monastic remains can often be exciting to explore, enthralling even the 'coolest' of youngsters, who, instead of having to be 'dragged' around such sites, can be involved and made an important part of the visit. They will, in particular, I hope, enjoy the challenge of 'finding', in secluded corners or high up on a wall, strange carvings such as saints' heads or grotesque gargoyles, or imagining castles under siege. If you make such places interesting for them, retelling stories about the battles and intrigues of the past, you will open their eyes in the best possible way to our turbulent history. I have also included places on some tours that cater primarily for children, but I think parents will not be able to resist joining in.

Although not on a comparable scale to other countries, we are fortunate here in Ireland that a good number of our great houses have survived our recent past: once the property of the élite, many of these are now owned by the State and can be enjoyed by all. Similarly, elaborate and extensive gardens—the intricate interplay of man's ingenuity and nature on a grand scale, jewels in our landscape originally laid out by seventeenth- and eighteenth-century plantsmen—are now available to all.

Whether in the more formal forest parks or on the hills and mountains around Dublin, there is a wealth of fascinating flora and fauna waiting to be discovered.

I have included some provincial towns and villages on the routes: take the time to enjoy their easier pace of life and, indeed, the fresh, keenly priced produce of their butchers and greengrocers!

While each Day Tour has a goal destination, the routes to and from that destination are selected to provide interesting but optional stops 'along the way'. Where there is more than plenty to do to fill the day at the main destination itself, a direct, major road route is chosen going and/or returning, otherwise routes along mainly quiet country roads are recommended. The ultimate destinations of all these Day Tours are within a maximum of one-and-a-half hours' drive from the M50 motorway that encircles Dublin, which, for simplicity, is chosen as the starting point of every tour. The time it takes to complete these tours will depend very much on the level of your interest in the different places featured; in some cases you may find it difficult to cover all of the locations in one day, and may have to return for a second visit. Distances given, and kilometre/mileage comparisons, are approximate.

As some of the places, particularly the ruined castles and churches I recommend visiting, are little-known and out-of-the-way, they are in their original, untouched, ruined state, not 'prettified' by the OPW, without handrails, easy steps or paths, and often without significant interference since the time they became ruined, centuries ago. Because of their untouched state, they are often more evocative of the past than ruins that have been 'taken into care'. In some cases, their condition means they have to be visited with due care, and might not be suitable for young children. It is worthwhile bringing boots if you are going to explore such sites. I have not included any sites where access appeared to be a problem, but if in doubt, do enquire locally and ask permission, if necessary. We owe our thanks to landowners who allow the curious to cross their land to access such monuments.

Apart from these everyday heritage sites, which can be visited without charge, I also include some places, such as Emo Court and Glendalough Visitors' Centre, which are in the care of Dúchas, The Heritage Service of Ireland. The purchase of a Heritage Card from Dúchas will allow you unlimited admission for one year to their sites all over the country (sixty-five in all) for € 20; a senior citizen's ticket costs € 15; children/students a mere € 7.50; and a family ticket is € 50. For more information telephone 01 6472461, or e-mail *heritagecard@duchas.ie*.

I hope you enjoy the country around Dublin as much as I did while researching this book. And remember, on quiet country roads, do take great care to drive at a leisurely pace.

Michael Fewer
February 2006

KEY MAP

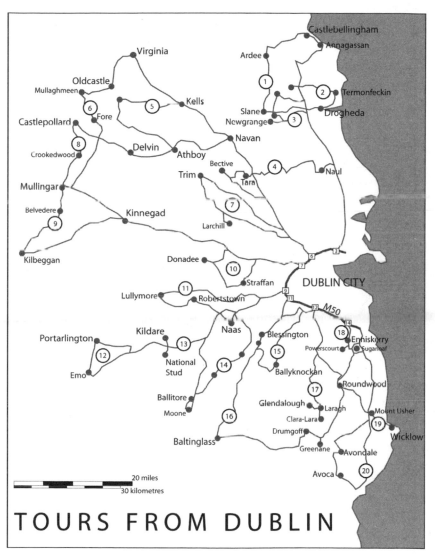

TOURS FROM DUBLIN

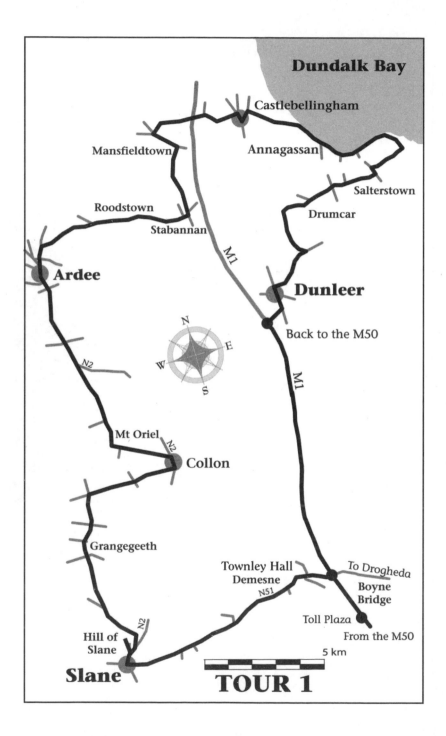

Dundalk Bay

Castlebellingham

Mansfieldtown

Annagassan

Salterstown

Roodstown

Drumcar

Stabannan

M1

Ardee

Dunleer

Back to the M50

N

E

W

S

M1

N2

Mt Oriel

N2

Collon

Grangegeeth

Townley Hall
Demesne

To Drogheda

N51

Boyne
Bridge

N2

Toll Plaza

From the M50

Hill of
Slane

5 km

Slane

TOUR 1

TOUR 1

Slane, Co. Meath, and a little-known corner of Co. Louth
✤

This tour visits the pretty village of Slane, touches on the River Boyne and views the legendary Hill of Slane before taking a long loop through some little-known, but fascinating areas of County Louth.

ROUTE: **The M1 and N51 are taken to Slane, then the route mainly follows side roads through County Louth, rejoining the M1 south of Dunleer for the journey home.**

DISTANCE: **177km (110 miles).**

MAPS: **OS Discovery numbers 50, 43 and primarily 36.**

Leave the M50 (northbound) at intersection 3 and head north on the M1. After 32km (20 miles) you pass through the M1 toll (fee: €1.60). Crossing the fine suspension bridge over the River Boyne about 40km (25 miles) from the M50, take the next exit, signposted N51, for Slane and Drogheda North. At the roundabout, turn left for Slane: within a few minutes you will pass the site of the Battle of the Boyne at Oldbridge, on the left, followed by the steep, wooded hillside demesne of Townley Hall, on the right. At about 8km (5 miles) from the M1 you will get a glimpse of the great green dome of the Knowth Neolithic monument, over to the left.

As you approach the village of Slane, on your right-hand side look out for the little slated cottage that was the home of the poet Francis Ledwidge (1887–1917). It is open to the public all year round: 10.00am–1.00pm and 2.00pm–6.00pm, adults €2.50, children €1. The cottage and the garden behind it are filled with memorabilia and displays honouring this gifted poet who died in the trenches during the First World War. Ledwidge was already writing poetry when he left school at the age of thirteen, and continued to do so while he worked locally as a labourer; his first published work appeared in the *Drogheda Independent* in 1912. He came to the attention of Lord Dunsany, dramatist and writer, who called him 'the poet of the blackbird' and arranged the publication of a book of his poetry, *Songs of the Field*. By then, however, like many young men of his generation, Ledwidge had joined the Army. He saw action at Gallipoli, in the Balkans and in France before he was killed at Ypres, in Belgium, in July 1917.

A short distance further on from the cottage you enter the village of Slane: park as near the main crossroads in the village as possible. You can take a short stroll around the village, and perhaps a coffee in the Conyngham Arms hotel, or choose a longer walk, either down the banks of the Boyne towards Rosnaree, or uphill and out of the village to climb the Hill of Slane. If walking is not your preference, when you are leaving the village you can take in the latter by car.

Slane is a well-laid-out estate village of the late eighteenth century, located on what was at the time an important crossroads: the intersection of the Dublin–Derry and the Drogheda–Navan roads. The importance of this crossroads is marked by four elegant, three-storey Georgian houses, with flanking pavilions, set at an angle of 45° to the cross and forming an impressive octagon. These were built at different times during the 1760s and 1770s, the first—that on the north-east corner—being built as an inn. The rest of the village mainly comprises modest and typical nineteenth-century houses and shops, with some fine doorcases and window details.

The Church of Ireland Church of St Patrick dates from the late eighteenth century and has a few features of interest: just inside the gate, on the right, is an unusual bronze monument, like a miniature Roman temple, dedicated to Eva Amabel, who died in 1909. The western gable of the sacristy has a small but rich collection of ancient stones, including an elaborate coat of arms of the Barnwall family, who were very important in the eastern Pale area during the sixteenth and seventeenth centuries, and two Norman stone coffin lids, which are said to have been brought here for safe-keeping from ruined Stackallen church.

For those who would like a riverside walk—a stroll of a little more than an hour—go downhill from the village to the bridge and cross over to the south bank of the river, where there is a walkway. Alternatively, you can drive down and park in the car park below Fennor Church and Castle. Fennor Castle, built on a rocky outcrop overlooking the Boyne, is a later form of castle known as a fortified house, characterised by tall chimneys and large windows, in the centre of which the previous castle or towerhouse, with its battered base, can be seen.

At the river walk, cross a stile to reach the towpath of the Boyne canal and follow it eastwards. The Boyne navigation, built to link towns like Navan and Trim to the sea at Drogheda, was commenced in the mid-eighteenth century, with locks built at some sections to avoid the stretches of rapids on the river. Although regular passenger-ferrying and transport of goods did not cease until the early twentieth century, the venture was never a commercial success. The towpath can still be followed for a distance downstream, although it can be mucky underfoot and sometimes a little overgrown. You should make it as far as Rosnaree Lock, though, a sturdy example of canal engineering, before turning around and heading back. The legendary High King of Ireland, Cormac Mac Airt, asked that he be buried at Rosnaree rather than in the usual burial place of kings: Brú na Boinne. The druids thought otherwise, however, and set out to bury him at Brú na Boinne, but a flood arose on the river as they attempted to take the bier across, and the bier was swept away. The following morning it was found to have come ashore at Rosnaree, and Cormac was laid to rest there after all.

—⊷—

To get to the Hill of Slane, ascend Chapel Street from the crossroads. On the right is the Catholic church, an early modern structure erected about 1800: the freestanding round tower is said to be the first Catholic belfry erected in Meath since the Reformation. Such a large and visible Catholic church in a Protestant estate village—built with the use of a substantial donation from and on land donated by Earl Conyngham —is unusual for the time, but thereby hangs a good story. The parish priest, Fr O'Hanlon, who had been educated in France, was back there on a visit in 1796 and staying at the Irish College when he heard that Earl Conyngham had been arrested by the Paris Military Tribunal. He went to the Tribunal and interceded on the Earl's behalf—describing him as a model of liberality among the Irish aristocracy—and obtained his release. Later, on his return home, the Earl repaid the favour by making it possible for the new church to be built.

Take the first turn left, signed for the Hill of Slane, and in less than 1km (0.5 mile) the top of the hill is reached.

It is said that St Patrick 'fast-tracked' the winning-over of the pagan people of Ireland to the Christian religion by, sensibly, first converting their leaders: the many minor kings and chiefs who ruled in Ireland at the time. The foremost of these was the High King (*Ard Rí*), and at the season of Easter, which coincided with an important pagan spring festival, King Loiguire presided over a gathering on the Hill of Tara, the high point of which was the lighting of a great fire by the king.

It was the custom that no other celebratory fire could be lit until the king's fire was lit, and the penalty for premature kindling of a fire was death. Patrician tradition says St Patrick brought himself to the attention of the High King by doing just that: on the night of Easter Sunday in the year AD 432 he lit a Paschal fire on this hill, which lies some 16km (10 miles) distant from, and in full view of, the Hill of Tara. The High King took a force of twenty-seven chariots to the Hill of Slane to capture the law-breaker and put him to death. St Patrick put a curse on the approaching force and the chariots and their occupants were destroyed, with the exception of the king and his wife, who in this way were persuaded to become Christians.

St Patrick founded a monastery here that lasted well into the medieval period, in spite of attacks by the Vikings and the Dubliners, who burnt the round tower here in AD 948. There was probably a *rath* on the western side of the hill, on top of which the first Norman lord of Slane, Richard le Fleming, built a large motte and bailey, which can still be seen in the trees. As there are no traces surviving of the original monastery, this motte, dating from the 1170s, is the oldest structure in the area. The ruined buildings that crown the hill, which consist of a Franciscan college and a parish church dating from the fifteenth century, are rich in interesting decorative stone carvings and full of stairs, vaults, nooks and crannies that will appeal to young children.

The college, on the right, is a substantial affair consisting of three ranges surrounding a central cloister, although it is said to have housed just four priests, four lay brothers and four choristers. There is a remarkable number of large fireplaces, which must have kept the lay brothers busy, suggesting there was an abundant supply of firewood available at the time; there are few trees on the hill today. A decidedly scary stairway (not suitable for young children) takes you up to a high point from where the layout of the place is easily understood, and from where there are magnificent views down into the town of Slane, across to the Dublin Mountains to the south and of the Irish Sea to the east, which stretches silverly along the horizon.

Mounted on the walls are some interesting stone plaques. Over the entrance doorway is a very historic piece: a carved coat of arms that includes the lions of England and the *fleurs-de-lys* of France, which may date to the fourteenth century when the kings of England claimed the throne of France. Inside, and to the left of the entrance, in what was probably the friary refectory, a plaque depicting a dragon or a griffin can be seen on the gable wall. Near the north west corner of the cloisters is the coat of arms of the Flemings, who founded the friary.

The ruined parish church occupies a prominently oval enclosure, which might suggest the footprint of the original monastery. There is a

Stone head on church tower, Hill of Slane

stair climbing to the top of the tower that affords fantastic views, but it is often padlocked. To the south of the church is a strange, crude stone monument consisting of two triangular upright stones and known as the Bishop's Tomb. It is possible that it is a very early Christian grave or reliquary. In former times it was held in great reverence—at funerals, coffins were carried around it three times before burial.

Leaving the village of Slane, take the N2 northwards and take the second turn to the left (the first turn takes you up to the Hill of Slane), signed Grangegeeth. Two long, straight roads are followed and you pass through Grangegeeth cross. It is a strange name, and probably derived from *Grainseach na Gaoithe*, meaning 'the monastic farm of the monks'. About 1.5km (1 mile) past Grangegeeth church, on the right, take a right turn signposted for Collon and cross into County Louth. In the village of Collon take the left turn at the crossroads and drive for a few hundred metres up the N2, passing some quaint arts and crafts houses on the right. Take the first turn left, and a long straight road takes you up onto the flanks of Mount Oriel, which is topped with an array of telecommunications masts. As you bear right and descend the northern side of the hill a marvellous view opens up ahead of Slieve Gullion and the Cooley peninsula extending out into the Irish sea, and beyond, the southern summits of the Mourne Mountains peek over the top of Slieve Foy.

At the bottom of the hill rejoin the N2 and follow it into the town of Ardee. Where the road crosses the River Dee as it enters the town is the reputed location of the ford where, legend has it, the champion of Ulster, Cúchulainn, fought to the death with his friend and Connacht's champion, Ferdia. The combat is said to have lasted three days. In the end, Cúchulainn killed Ferdia with a magic spear. A bronze statue near the river commemorates the event.

Ardee is a Norman town and for a long time was a northern outlier of The Pale, occupying an important position as a staging-point for campaigns against the Ulster Irish. It was originally walled, but while little remains of the walls today, it is one of the few towns of the period where early towerhouses survive as part of the streetscape. These and the nineteenth-century houses and shops that line the main street make it an attractive place. In particular, before you reach the bridge look out, on the left, for Hamill's public house, which boasts a sumptuous, glazed tile façade, and you can't miss St Leger's Castle on the main street, the largest surviving fortified medieval townhouse in Ireland, which now serves periodically as a courthouse. Other buildings worth mentioning in the town are Hatch Castle, another fortified townhouse, and, as an example of what not to do, take a look at the former Catholic church in John Street. Before its conversion, this was a good example of an early post-Penal church, with fine late Georgian interiors.

If you wish to lunch in Ardee, there is a number of eating places. The Ferdia Arms serves up good, home-cooked meals, the quality of which seems to be confirmed by the number of locals who avail of takeaway Sunday dinners, plated and covered with tinfoil. If you are picnicking, it is worthwhile waiting until the tour reaches the coast at Annagassan.

———

Leaving Ardee, bear right at the northern end of the town, go straight through a roundabout and take the next turn right. A little over 3km (2 miles) out you will see Roodstown Castle on the left. It is worth gaining access, if even just to climb the stairs to the battlements. The keyholder is Michael MacMahon, who lives a couple of hundred metres further on, on the right, just beyond the grey gable of a cottage, and who is the proprietor of MacMahon's Garden Sheds (tel: 041 6853647). Be warned: this road must be the garden shed capital of Ireland —MacMahon's is one of about five shed purveyors along here!

Roodstown is a typical example of a well-preserved, fortified residence of a fifteenth-century landowner. Between 1420 and 1440 the government in Dublin offered a grant of £10 (a large sum of money at the time) towards the erection of towerhouses similar to this: it was obviously in their interests to have strong and secure landowners, particularly at the vulnerable boundaries of The Pale, which were always being pushed outwards. From the wall-walk of the castle the views are extensive, looking out towards the flatlands of County Louth to the north, where the unruly Irish still held on in the fifteenth and sixteenth centuries, and beyond to the Carlingford peninsula and the Mournes rising from Dundalk Bay. When I visited, a pair of great ravens were constructing a nest in one of the north windows, and they were not amused to be interrupted.

Continuing eastwards, the hamlet of Stabannan is reached after about 3km (2 miles): turn left after the Catholic church and drive north, with the very large demesne of Braganstown to the left, one of the largest areas of almost blank map you will find on the east coast. At the next T-junction, turn left. The gates to Braganstown are passed on the left, just before crossing the River Glyde, which rises in County Cavan and which we will meet later as it enters the sea at Annagassan. On the far side of the river the little graveyard around the ruined church is remarkable for the number of signs it has forbidding litter.

A couple of hundred metres on, at the crossroads, turn right onto the R166, which takes you over the M1 and into the village of Castlebellingham. A pretty village surrounding a triangular village green, it was for many years submerged in heavy traffic, but now that the M1 has taken most of the cars away there is hope that it can blossom again. It is a typical estate village of the kind common in England, with the big house (now a hotel) set back from the road behind a Victorian castellated gatehouse, and a fine village church and estate cottages. Beside the church is a group of magical *cottage orné* dating from the 1830s, with tall brick chimneys, flamboyant bargeboards and leaded windows. Some of them are in a 'tired' condition, but not too far gone to be rescued now that the plague of traffic is over. Another endearing feature of the village are the frequent blue-and-white ceramic glazed tiles and plaques mounted on the fronts and sides of some buildings, mostly portraying religious motifs or scenes.

From the village green, take the road signposted for Annagassan and in minutes the road takes you to the shores of the Irish Sea. There is a number of informal lay-bys where you can park and take in the fine view of the Carlingford peninsula across the expanse of Dundalk Bay. In winter and spring great numbers of geese and waders can be seen here along the shore: only on Strangford Lough and the Shannon estuary have more waders been counted. Thousands of golden plover, dunlin, knot, oystercatchers and lapwing roost along these shores, too, along with almost every species of duck and goose to be seen in Ireland.

Drive on south to cross the stone bridge into the village of Annagassan. In the shelter of Dunany Point, an estuary—where the salmon- and trout-rich rivers Glyde and Dee enter the sea—was occupied by an Irish tribe called the Fir Arda Cinnachta in the first millennium: a large ringwork known as Lios na Rann is pointed out as the site of their settlement. It became a favourite wintering place for the Vikings in the ninth century, and they eventually founded a permanent settlement here, only to be driven out by the native Irish in AD 928. It is not surprising, particularly given the proximity of the M1, that this area is now attracting apartment developments. For lunch, the Glyde Inn, a restaurant and B&B run by Ann and Paul O'Neill, has a good reputation.

Continue along the coast road, and when the main road goes right and inland, continue along the coast as the road narrows: there are many possibilities for a picnic spot along here. Eventually, about 4km (2.5 miles) from Annagassan the little coast road turns inland for the pleasant hamlet of Salterstown, where you turn left at the T-junction. Reaching the R116 a short distance on, turn left and almost immediately right to follow a side road towards Drumcar. Dillonstown church is passed on the left at Dillonstown cross: go straight through, taking care. Before long you will come upon the entrance to St Mary's Hospital, run by the St John of God Brothers and based around a fine and intact eighteenth-century house that was the seat of the McClintock family. A little further on is Drumcar church, hidden in the trees on the right but marked by a timber-framed, terracotta-tiled lychgate. The church itself is a simple neo-Gothic building dating to the 1840s. Behind it lies the old pre-Penal church and a fine McClintock mausoleum: an octagonal chapel in the Gothic style built in 1858.

Follow the road as it swings left after Drumcar church, and turn right at the next T-junction to descend under a railway bridge and enter the village of Dunleer. Go south through the village and take the first right to reach the M1 and return to Dublin.

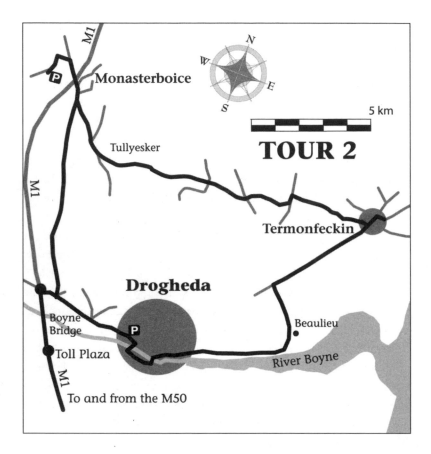

TOUR 2

5 km

M1

Monasterboice

Tullyesker

M1

Termonfeckin

Drogheda

Boyne
Bridge

Toll Plaza

M1

To and from the M50

Beaulieu

River Boyne

Drogheda, Beaulieu, Termonfeckin and Monasterboice

〜ℓℓ

This route brings you to the historic town of Drogheda, and on a circuit that takes in a mansion of the eighteenth century, a towerhouse of the fifteenth century and decorated High Crosses of the early Christian period.

ROUTE: The M1 and N51 are followed to Drogheda, then the route follows minor roads out along the River Boyne and north to Termonfeckin. The route then turns east to reach Monasterboice, before returning to Dublin by the M1.

DISTANCE: 142km (90 miles).

MAPS: OS Discovery numbers 36, 50 and mainly 43.

Exit the M50 at intersection 3 for the M1 and head north, out of County Dublin and into County Meath. A toll plaza is located 32km (20 miles) north: the toll fee is €1.60 each way. About 40km (25 miles) from the M50 is an off-ramp signposted for Slane and Drogheda North; leave the motorway and take the N51 into Drogheda. As you drive downhill into the town, follow the first signs that you see directing you to a large car park, which should be that located in Bolton Square, behind the Corporation Buildings on Fair Street.

Situated on the River Boyne, about 7km (4 miles) from the sea, Drogheda was probably first established by the Norsemen as a trading and wintering-over base. Early in the Norman occupation of Ireland Hugh de Lacy built a massive motte castle here, which still dominates the south bank of the Boyne and overlooks the town, and is today topped by a Martello tower and home to the Millmount Museum and

Craft Centre. Throughout the Middle Ages, Drogheda remained an important English town and port and a number of parliaments met here. The darkest hour for the town came in 1649 when it was besieged by the forces of Oliver Cromwell and defended by a mainly English loyalist garrison. On 10 September, after a heavy cannon bombardment, the Cromwellians successfully stormed the town, whereupon thousands of the defenders were put to death and the survivors transported to Barbados.

Today, Drogheda is a rare mix of new and old. Although recent years have brought much renewal to the town in the form of fine modern buildings, a good stock of Georgian pedimented doorcases and delicate fanlights of ashlar limestone and intricate wrought iron survive to invoke the past. Between the main streets is a network of old-world, narrow alleyways and winding flights of steps that add considerably to the character of the town, which is full of pleasant visual surprises, such as the 'drive-through' Augustinian Abbey off Dominic Street, or the art gallery in the old Franciscan church off Laurence Street, which you enter at first-floor level.

For a short tour of the town, leave Bolton Square, walk downhill past the side of the Corporation Buildings and turn left onto Fair Street. Every variety of Georgian doorcase and fanlight is to be seen along this street. At the end of the street, on the right, is Patrick Clarke's pub, a rare example of a genuine old pub, with snugs sporting benches and screens with comb-marked varnish finish, and where an ancient clock ticks away the quiet hours—and the Guinness is good.

Diagonally across the street from Clarke's is St Peter's Church of Ireland, the robust classical tower and spire of which dominate the north-east corner of the town. The building stands on the site of an earlier, more extensive church, which dated from the thirteenth century and housed as many as seven separate chapels. It was also reputed to have the highest steeple in Christendom, which was blown down in a storm in 1549. In 1649, as Drogheda fell to Cromwell, a group of townspeople took refuge in the church, only to be burned to death when it was set on fire by the Puritan soldiers. The present church, with its fine palladian limestone façade, was designed by the architect Hugh Darley and dates from 1748, while the tower and spire, by Francis

Johnson, date from 1780. The interior is decorated with some wonderful late baroque plasterwork and elaborate memorial monuments. A stroll around the churchyard is recommended: see if you can find the grave of a member of the Duggan family who survived the Charge of the Light Brigade during the Crimean War. Mounted on the cemetery wall in the north-east corner is a reminder of mortality: the carved stone lid that formerly covered the tomb of Sir Edmund Golding and his wife, dating from about 1520, and depicting the couple's decomposing corpses.

Walk down Peter Street towards the river. Ahead you will see the former Tholsel, topped by a fine clock-tower and dating from 1770, and beyond it, on the far side of the river, the elegant, pinnacled spire of St Mary's Church of Ireland, now no longer in use. The pleasant chimes you hear in the centre of Drogheda every fifteen minutes emanate from the clock of the old Tholsel, now housing offices of the Bank of Ireland. Turn left up Laurence Street to see Laurence's Gate. Before the gate and on the left, set back from the street and, at time of writing, now derelict, is the former Methodist chapel featuring windows of very elaborate sandstone, Gothic tracery; one hopes this disregarded old building will find a suitable new use. Further on, unconvincing modern Georgiana replaces two fine buildings shamefully demolished as late as 1989: the Free School of 1728 and Mr Singleton's house of 1740. Laurence Gate and the fragment of town wall beside it are imposing reminders of the importance of Drogheda in medieval times. The base of the double-towered gateway dates from the thirteenth century, while the upper sections were added at various times up to the fifteenth century.

Return back along Laurence Street and turn left, onto Shop Street, to cross St Mary's Bridge. On the far side of James' Street (perpendicular to Shop Street) is a pedestrian alleyway that leads to Duleek Street, off which is Millmount Museum, originally a fort centred around Hugh de Lacy's great motte. The fort came under Cromwell's cannon-fire in 1649, and the Martello tower built atop the motte during the Napoleonic Wars was damaged by shellfire during the Civil War in 1923. De Lacy's motte is said to have been built upon a far more ancient burial mound, representing the oldest man-made structure in Drogheda. The Museum is housed in the former officers' quarters of Richmond Fort: the entire complex was restored by the Corporation as a millennium project, and the museum includes a unique collection of finely embroidered pictorial guild and trade parade banners. The Martello Tower itself houses an exhibition of Drogheda's military history (opening hours: Monday–Saturday, 10.00am–6.00pm; Sunday and Bank Holidays, 2.30pm–5.30pm. Admission: adults €5.50; children and OAPs €3; family rate €12).

Return across the River Boyne back into Shop Street and take the second turn left into West Street. Dominating the north side of the street is the Roman Catholic St Peter's Church, which dates from the end of the nineteenth century and replaces an older building by Francis Johnson. The interior is typically busy and garish late nineteenth-century Gothic, and boasts the elaborate Gothic shrine of St Oliver Plunkett, in which his mummified head is displayed. Oliver Plunkett was born in 1654 in County Meath to an old English Catholic family. As was common during the time of the Penal Laws in Ireland, he was sent to Europe to be educated and was ordained a priest in Rome. He returned to Ireland in 1670 as Archbishop of Armagh, but was arrested in 1678 and put on trial for instigating a popish plot. Found guilty on the evidence of witnesses who were notoriously unreliable, he was executed by being hanged, drawn and quartered. He was declared a saint by Pope Paul VI in 1973. The door of the cell in which he was imprisoned in Newgate, London, is also on display in the church.

Leave the church and turn right. Return to Bolton Square by taking the next turn to the right, which brings you back onto Fair Street.

If you want to lunch in Drogheda before continuing our tour, Monk's Coffee Bar, next to The Wise Owl bookshop on the corner of South Quay and St Mary's Bridge, is a good place for a light lunch; it also offers 'upmarket' takeaways of bruschettas, paninis and sandwiches. Another recommended place is Jaffa's restaurant in Fitzwilliam Court, off Dyer Street (parallel to West Street). It has a selection of paninis, wraps and ciabattas plus a fine terrace for alfresco dining, overlooking the Boyne and the south bank.

To depart from Drogheda you must cross the Boyne twice: leave Bolton Square car park and descend to cross the river over the Bridge of Peace at the bottom of George's Street. Follow the dual carriageway to St Mary's Bridge and turn left to cross back over the river, turning right on the far side along the North Quay and following a sign for Baltray. Take the second left, again following the signs for Baltray, then first right and soon after you will drive under the towering railway viaduct.

The Normans built the first bridge at Drogheda on the site of a ford, which gave the town its name: Droichead Átha, or ford bridge. However, the steep gorge and broad estuary of the Boyne posed a major challenge to the engineers building the Belfast–Dublin railway line in the 1840s: the soft clays in and around the Boyne would not take the weight of a stone bridge. The problem was solved when Dundalk engineer John MacNeill envisaged limiting the use of stone to the piers, which would carry a novel cast-iron lattice structure to take the railway. The bridge, which utilised the longest lattice construction of its type in the world, opened in April 1855. In the 1930s the cast-iron structure was replaced by a steel lattice, but otherwise the great bridge remains unaltered.

The road passes through Drogheda's port and emerges beside the sloblands of the Boyne Estuary, on which a range of wildfowl, including widgeon and waders, can be seen at low tide. Just over 3km (2 miles) from the centre of Drogheda take a turn left away from the shore, and ahead of you in the trees you will see Beaulieu House and the little church on its grounds.

A picturesque, crumbling brick demesne wall steps up the hill to the white entrance gates, beyond which the house stands at the end of a short avenue. At time of writing the house and gardens are open Monday–Friday, 11.00am–5.00pm, June–September; weekends are reserved for coach tours and groups. The entrance fee for the house and gardens is €10, and €5 for the gardens only. I would recommend that you telephone ahead to confirm opening times (tel: 041 9832265).

Beaulieu House is one of my favourite Irish houses: I like the warmth lent to its elevations by the red-brick-lined windows and main door, its comfortable interior scale and its very lived-in ambiance. It really doesn't look Irish at all and certainly would not be out of place in northern France, Belgium, or Holland. Although long thought to have been built in the 1660s, recent research seems to suggest that what you see today is, in all probability, the result of extensive rebuilding work carried out between 1710 and 1720 by Henry Tichbourne, Lord Ferrard, to an early seventeenth-century Plunkett house designed by the architect John Curle.

In spite of the years that have passed and the many minor alterations that have taken place, much of the original interior decoration has survived. My favourite room is the entrance hall: a double-height space with walls adorned with landscape paintings and Tichbourne portraits and furnished with an eclectic collection of fine chairs, tables and bits and pieces collected over the years. The arched doorways off the hall have wonderful spandrel panels of intricately carved arms and military trophies. The carpet on the floor and the curtains beside the main door are comfortably frayed, and the place smells old and warm and lived-in.

In the gardens of the house stands an old church. It is a plain building of the early nineteenth century, but if you can arrange it, obtain the key to gain access and get a look at the two ancient grave-slabs that used to be fixed to the outside walls. One is a gruesome cadaver grave-slab depicting a female corpse in an advanced stage of decomposition and featuring toads, lizards, worms and newts. It is thought that this slab may commemorate a victim of the plague that swept across the east of Ireland in the 1440s. The other slab, with its simple decoration of a foliated cross, is probably earlier and of Norman date.

The garden is a walled space terraced towards the south and filled with an amazing variety of plants. There is no formality about it, and it sort of mirrors the diversity of the interiors of the house in a haphazard riot of colour and form. At the highest level is a huge, colourful border of familiar and not-so-familiar plants, many twice the size I am accustomed to seeing them, and mixed together with the colourful stems, leaves and blossoms of exotic plants. At the lower levels the garden seamlessly becomes a fruit and kitchen garden; the whole place is a marvellous celebration of plantsmanship.

Leaving Beaulieu, turn right outside the gates and drive north; after 1.5km (1 mile), turn right again for the village of Termonfeckin, nearly 3km (2 miles) away. It is a very pleasant village and was once a place of ecclesiastical importance. St Fechin established a monastery here in the seventh century, and in the Middle Ages it was a seat of the Anglo-Irish Archbishop of Armagh. The Ecclesiastical Courts of Armagh were held for a long time in Drogheda, and when the Primate was in residence in Termonfeckin the courts moved there with him. There is a record of a public penance meted out to a local resident who was convicted by the court of perjury: he had to 'walk around the cemetery clothed in white linen on six different Sundays, and to fast on bread and water for three days.' Little remains of the old Termonfeckin, however, other than a badly eroded High Cross in the grounds of St Fechin's Church of Ireland. Just over 1.5km (1 mile) east of the village is a sandy beach that stretches for miles, northwards towards Clogher Head and southwards towards Baltray and the famous golf course.

In Termonfeckin, hidden away down a side road, you will find an almost intact towerhouse castle. Take the second turn right (east) from the main road through the village (signposted for Clogher Head) and turn right again after a couple of hundred metres, taking a left a little further on. The little castle is at the end of a narrow cul-de-sac. The key giving access to it can be obtained from the house on the left, at the end of the road, opposite the castle.

Built in the fifteenth century and extensively repaired in 1641, the castle is in very good order and still roofed. The structure is unique in that, while the first floor is vaulted, as is common for towerhouses, the top floor has a stone slab corbelled floor, similar to the structure used in the great tomb at Newgrange. A narrow spiral staircase takes you to the battlemented roof, from which it can be seen that the structure stands on a raised mound and there may well have once been an outer defensive wall.

Return to the main road and turn left. Take the first right, and after nearly 2.4km (1.5 miles) turn left and then right. Follow the road straight towards Tullyesker for nearly 6.4km (4 miles) to reach the R132. Turn right and after nearly 3km (1.8 miles) you reach and pass under the M1, following signs for Monasterboice, less than 1km (0.5 mile) west of the motorway. There is a car park and toilets beside the relatively small site, and a kiosk where literature can be obtained; the kiosk is operated on a voluntary basis and although entry to the site is free, donations are welcomed.

The original monastery here was founded by St Buithe, who is recorded as having died in AD 521. While none of the original buildings remains, we know from the remains of earthen embankments that were discovered through aerial photography that the original enclosure was as much as nineteen acres in extent, and of course the quality and size of the monuments associated with the monastery—the two great High Crosses and the round tower—are also indications that this was a very important place in the first millennium.

As you enter the graveyard and pass by a yew tree, you are confronted by the massive Muiredach's Cross, standing 5.5m high and covered with some of the finest stone-carved decoration of any cross of its type and date, which is reckoned to be tenth century. Wonderfully and simply depicted are many scenes from the Old and New Testament, together with images of animals and zoomorphic designs. You do have to look carefully, but you should have no difficulty identifying scenes such as Adam and Eve, with the apple, beside Cain striking Able, the adoration of the Magi and the arrest of Christ. At low level, near children's eye level, on the west face, you will find two cats playing with their prey, a bird and a frog.

Beyond are the shells of two surviving churches, the nearest with a possible twelfth-century date and the other, slightly bigger church dating from the late thirteenth or early fourteenth century. The round tower, the roof and bellcote, which were probably destroyed by lightning, is at least 1,000 years old. What does remain stands at a height of 34m. Strangely, the Norsemen never sacked the monastery of Monasterboice, as they did practically every other Irish monastery, but it was comprehensively plundered by the Irish. The annals record that it was attacked by the forces of the High King in 968, when 300 monks were herded into one of the buildings and burnt alive. It is further recorded that the round tower was burnt, together with the books and the monastic treasures it contained, in the year 1097.

Beside the second church stands what is known as the West Cross— tall and slender in comparison to Muiredach's Cross and considerably more weathered. Among the scenes decoratively depicted are the Resurrection and the sacrifice of Isaac. In the north-east corner of the churchyard is a third cross, but this is very eroded and less decorated than the other two.

To return to Dublin, return to the M1 and head south.

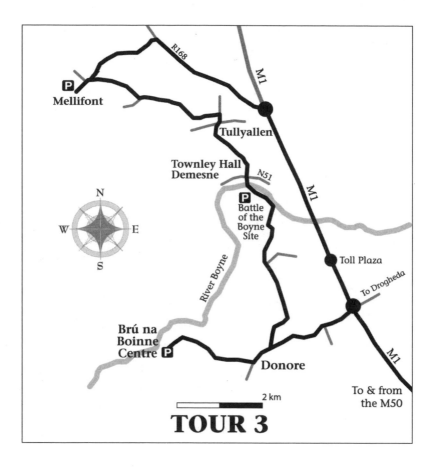

TOUR 3

TOUR 3

Newgrange, Knowth, Mellifont and the Battle of the Boyne

≫

This tour takes you to some of the oldest and most dramatic Neolithic monuments in Ireland, if not Europe, to the remains of the first Cistercian monastery built in Ireland, and to the site of one of the most important European battles of the early modern period: the Battle of the Boyne.

ROUTE: **The M1 takes you north speedily, and the rest of the route is quiet side roads to the west, finishing with a return again by the M1.**

DISTANCE: **100km (62 miles).**

MAPS: **OS Discovery numbers 50 and mainly 43.**

Exit the M50 at intersection 3 onto the M1 and head north. Nearly 32km (20 miles) north the toll plaza is reached (fee: €1.60), after which you leave the M1 at the exit for Drogheda and Donore, about 38km (24 miles) from the M50. Follow the signs for Donore and turn right in the village opposite the church. Passing Daly's pub, begin a gentle descent into the valley of the River Boyne, and 1.6km (1 mile) from the village turn right into the gates of Brú na Boinne Interpretive Centre.

It should be noted that while the Ordnance map (Discovery 43) suggests that the road along the north of the Boyne is the best way to get to Newgrange and there is a car park indicated at the site, you will be turned away at the entrance kiosk. In spite of its seeming remoteness from them (Newgrange is more than 2km (1 mile), and Knowth more than 3km (1.8 miles) from the Interpretive Centre), the tombs at Newgrange and Knowth *can only be visited from the Interpretive Centre.* The centre is open all year round: for details telephone 041 9880305.

The remoteness of the centre from the tombs means you have to take shuttle buses. These depart at specific times to and from the tombs, which means you may spend some time waiting your turn. It takes approximately three-and-a-half hours to visit the two monuments, Newgrange and Knowth, but some of the waiting time can be spent watching a video about the sites, browsing in the bookshop or eating in the cafeteria, which serves a range of food from sandwiches to microwaved meals. You can opt to visit both monuments, or either one or the other. I have to say both are worth seeing and are different enough from each other to make the two trips from the centre worthwhile. The cost to visit the two monuments is €9.75.

A word of warning: you have to leave the centre and cross a footbridge over the Boyne and then walk up to the bus stop, so be sure you allow yourself time to catch your bus.

The great tomb at Newgrange is a most imposing and spectacular sight, and the guides who take you around and into it are very good. This monument was constructed by a Neolithic civilisation 5,000 years ago—500 years before the great pyramids of Giza were built and 1,000 years before the erection of Stonehenge in England. The Neolithic peoples arrived in Ireland about 6,000 years ago and began clearing the primeval forests to create suitable land for crops and grazing. The soil was particularly good along the River Boyne, and the people who settled here prospered. In time they were able to generate sufficient surpluses to allow the diversion of labour towards religion and culture: they could afford to devote some of their workforce to the building of funerary monuments, such as court tombs and portal dolmens. Over a long period of time their increasing prosperity, together with their knowledge of the seasons in relation to the sun and moon and their religious aspirations, led to the construction of a series of unique and major monuments along the Boyne. Forty of these monuments survive today, the greatest of which are the passage tombs of Newgrange, Knowth and Dowth, all within a few kilometres of one another.

Newgrange is the largest of the Boyne tombs, consisting of a mound of earth and stone 85m in diameter and 12m high, inside which a narrow, 22m-long, stone slab-lined passage leads to a corbelled chamber 6m high. Leading off this chamber are three alcoves, and when excavated each was found to contain human remains. The most remarkable feature of this structure is that it was constructed in such a way that on 21 December each year, the Winter Solstice, the rising sun shines directly through a small opening over the entrance and down the passage, suffusing the chamber in light. This phenomenon is artificially demonstrated to visitors throughout the year, but the real event attracts large crowds to Newgrange on mid-winter's day.

While the great passage grave at Newgrange stands on an open hill in isolated splendour, Knowth is surrounded by a series of seventeen 'mini-Knowths'—satellite tombs built at later times. Most of the giant kerbstones that originally retained the earthen mound are richly decorated with carved designs of spirals, lozenges and swirls, and there are so many such stones that they amount to one-third of all such Neolithic carvings discovered to date in Europe. These boulders, each weighing four tons or more, were brought all the way from the region of Clogher Head, 18km (11 miles) away. In all, about 1,600 boulders, ranging in weight from one to four or five tons, were used in the construction of the main mound at Knowth. This monument is also particularly interesting in that during the excavations archaeologists found evidence that occupation of the site continued from Neolithic times through the Iron Age, the early Christian period and into the Norman period. The site is much less pristine or 'tidied up' than that of Newgrange, and is scattered with partially excavated structures and tombs and therefore, for me, had a lot more atmosphere and was much more interesting. There are two long, narrow passages under the main mound at Knowth, but only part of one is accessible and features in the guided tour, although you can take photos in the passage, something you cannot do in Newgrange.

When you leave the Brú na Boinne Centre, turn left and head back for the village of Donore. Just beyond Donore, turn left at a thatched cottage and follow the sign for 'Battle of the Boyne'. The road winds northward and descends into the Boyne valley; there is a number of junctions along the way, but the Battle site is well signposted. About 3km (1.8 miles) from the thatched cottage you reach a T-junction, with a sign indicating that Tullyallen and Slane are to the left: go left and parallel to the Boyne canal for a couple of hundred metres to reach the gates to Oldbridge House. On the left is the entrance and car park for the Battle of the Boyne site (email: *battleoftheboyne@ealga.ie*). At time of writing (mid-2005) entry to the site, including guided tours, was free but there are plans to develop the site further, which may eventually lead to a tariff being imposed.

The Battle of the Boyne (1690), during which the forces of a deposed English king fought those of a newly crowned English king, was not only a major event in the history of Ireland but very significant in political and religious terms on the broader European stage. When James II's support in England collapsed, in part due to his pro-Catholic policies, he turned to France and Louis XIV for help. Although Catholic France was still regarded by most English people as the arch-enemy, James had spent much of his youth in France and had fought with the French Army. But Catholic Spain and the Holy Roman Empire sided with his Protestant opponent, William, formerly William of Orange, a Dutch prince. The Pope refused aid to James II because of his alliance with Louis XIV, who was at the time at loggerheads with the papacy. To complicate matters even further, it was a family affair: William was not only James' nephew but the husband of Mary, James' daughter.

William led a mixed and experienced army of 36,000 Dutch, German, Danish, Huguenot and English soldiers against James' inexperienced army of about 25,000 men, but the Jacobite forces had the advantage of being dug into excellent positions on the south bank of the Boyne. On 30 June 1690 William's forces arrived on the north banks of the Boyne, where James had decided to put an end to their advance into Ireland. With his army concealed in a deep ravine north of the river, which is today called King William's Glen, the Dutchman went forward with his officers to inspect the crossing places and the configuration of the Jacobite army. A ricochet from a lucky cannon shot from the south bank knocked William from his horse, wounding him slightly. On the south side of the Boyne the word spread that he had been killed, and it travelled all the way to Paris, where the guns of the Bastille were fired in triumph.

In fact, William shrugged off his mishap and the following morning, 1 July 1690, he led his army into battle. Diagrams displayed at the battle site show how the two forces were manoeuvred during the course of the battle, and numerous songs and poems tell of the bravery on both sides. Late in the afternoon, James—who had spent the day not on the field of battle, like William, but praying in the chapel in Donore—fled the Williamites' advance with a bodyguard of 300 horse, arriving in Dublin at 9.00pm that evening. It was not a greatly decisive battle in military terms—most of the Irish withdrew in some order to fight another day, leaving about 1,300 dead to the 400 dead of the Williamites. The propaganda effect on the Jacobite cause was devastating, however, and the echoes of the Battle of the Boyne can be heard even to this day.

Although the use of cavalry meant the extent of the actual battlefield was considerable, most of the ground—over 500 acres—is now in the ownership of the Irish State and work is proceeding to develop paths and information boards that will allow the interested visitor to follow the events of the battle step by step. At time of writing, 30–45 minute guided tours of the battlefield are available. The guides show the types of cannon, musket and sword used by the soldiers: this particularly appeals to children, who are fascinated by the weight of the 6lb cannonballs used extensively during the battle. Toilets and a picnic area are also provided at the site.

Drive out the gate of the battle site and turn left, then immediately swing right over the Boyne Canal and follow the road around to reach the River Boyne. Work on the Boyne Canal began in 1748, bypassing the rapids of the river to link prosperous towns such as Navan and Trim with the port of Drogheda and the sea. As with other Irish canals, the scheme was not a commercial success and regular passenger-ferrying and the transport of goods ceased in the early twentieth century. The towpaths are still walkable, however, for much of the way from Drogheda to Trim.

Cross over the bridge and keep straight on, crossing the main road. The road rises up through a deep, tree-shaded and steep-sided glen, with the Townley Hall demesne to the left. The glen has been called King William's Glen since 1690 because it was here the Williamite army concealed themselves before the Battle of the Boyne. Go straight through the next crossroads, and after a couple of hundred metres take the next turn left. A winding road takes you over Louth Hill and down into the valley of the River Mattock; turn left at the next crossroads to reach Mellifont Abbey.

A car park and picnic tables overlook the site, and across the road is a small visitors' centre that has a permanent exhibition of many beautiful stone fragments from the site. A guided tour of the abbey costs €2, and a family ticket is €5.50.

In AD 1140 St Malachy, then Bishop of Down, visited St Bernard in the Cistercian monastery of Clairveaux in France and was so impressed with what he saw of the work and organisation of the monks there that he resolved to bring the order to Ireland. On his return home he selected this site in the quiet valley of the Mattock, which belonged to his friend, Donnchadh O Cearbhaill, the local chief, for the first Cistercian monastery in Ireland. Monks arrived soon after from France and work began on building the monastery. By AD 1152 it was sufficiently complete to host the Synod of Drogheda.

The monks of Mellifont developed agriculture, horticulture and the salmon fisheries on the Boyne on a very large scale. At the height of its influence Mellifont Abbey owned 40,000 acres of land north and south of the river. The Cistercians' success in the development of the landscape and the revenues they generated greatly influenced other Irish chieftains, who sought monks to establish similar monasteries in their territories; within a decade of the completion of Mellifont, its monks had founded seven further abbeys in Ireland.

The ruins of Mellifont are very fragmentary. At the dissolution of the monasteries it became the residence of the Earl of Drogheda and suffered many attacks by Irish rebels. In the wars of 1640 it was besieged a number of times. After the Battle of the Boyne it fell into ruin, and gradually was quarried to provide stone for houses and walls for miles around. The remains of only two of the original buildings have survived to any extent: the Lavabo and the Gatehouse. The Lavabo, or monastery 'Washing Fountain', is the only one of its type extant in Ireland and is still, even in its ruinous state, a structure of beauty, with its sandstone arches and delicate pilasters with capitals ornamented with carved foliage.

Leaving the abbey, keep on straight for about 1.2km (0.75 mile) to reach the R168, and turn right. Soon you reach the M1 again north of the Boyne, and head southwards across the impressive suspension bridge and back to Dublin.

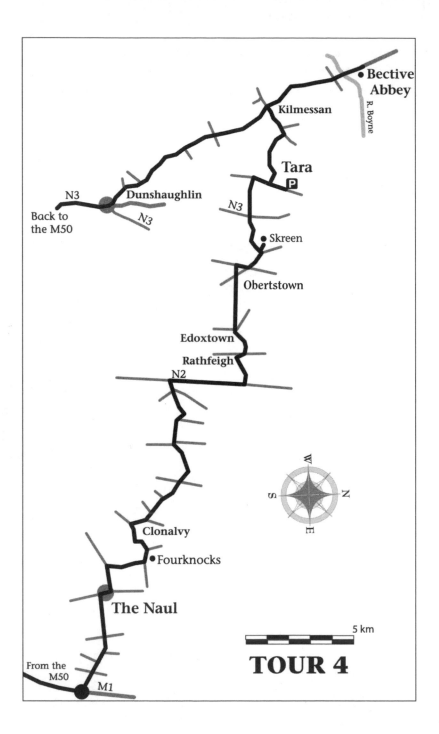

Bective
Abbey

R. Boyne

Kilmessan

Tara
P

N3

Dunshaughlin

N3

Back to
the M50

Skreen

Obertstown

Edoxtown

Rathfeigh

N2

Clonalvy

Fourknocks

The Naul

From the
M50

M1

5 km

TOUR 4

TOUR 4

Fourknocks, Tara and Bective Abbey

꧁

This tour includes the birthplace of a great piper, a 5,000-year-old burial place, the legendary Tara of the High Kings and a Cistercian abbey that became a great manor house.

ROUTE: The M1 is followed north, then drive along quiet side roads via Naul and Fourknocks to Tara and Bective Abbey. The return journey is made via Kilmessan to the N3 at Dunshaughlin, and from there return to Dublin.

DISTANCE: 128km (80 miles).

MAPS: OS Discovery numbers 50, 42 and mainly 43.

Take intersection 3 off the M50 to join the M1 northbound. About 19km (12 miles) to the north, leave the M1 at a sign for The Naul and a country road takes you to the quiet Fingal village in under 5.6km (3.5 miles).

On the right, just before entering The Naul, is an ancient church that has been in a state of sorry ruin since about AD 1630. It has a fine hooded ogee east window and a decorative Gothic west doorway. A stone plaque states that it was put into use again in AD 1710 as a burial place for the Hussey family of nearby Westown. The Naul is a pretty place: the village pub, Killian's, has a most unusual façade with a semi-circular pediment and is refreshingly without much in the way of advertising signs to indicate that it is a drink emporium. There is a particularly nice Cultural Centre on the left as you enter the village, with a cosy coffee shop that serves substantial snacks and lunches. Outside the centre, in the shade of a chestnut tree, you will find a statue of Seamus Ennis (1919–1982), piper, storyteller, folk music collector and broadcaster, who was born here.

Take the turn right in front of Killian's pub, and then immediately left at the bridge. After nearly 2km (about 1 mile), take the turn right, following the signs for Fourknocks, leaving County Dublin behind and entering County Meath. At a T-junction a little further on, turn left: after a couple of hundred metres you can park at the roadside opposite the entrance to Fourknocks, a Neolithic burial ground.

The key that opens the gate into the tomb is available locally; consult the sign inside the hedge as to where it can currently be obtained. A well-maintained gravel path takes you up the short distance to Fourknocks 1, the main tomb of a group of three burial monuments on this east–west ridge 152m above sea level. Inside the earth-covered tomb a passage leads to a large chamber, 6m in diameter, which appears, from archaeological evidence, to have been constructed in timber originally. The tomb is mainly comprised of limestone boulders, but contains some stones of grey shale, contrasting with the limestone, on which are carved typical Neolithic decorations of lozenges and chevrons. Uniquely, on one stone just left of the entrance a comical face is depicted. The tomb was excavated in 1950, when the remains of more than sixty-five men, women and children were uncovered, together with pottery and jewellery. Outside, a few stone steps lead up to the top of the steep-sided mound, from where the views are fine, taking in the Dublin Mountains to the south, the Irish Sea to the east and the Cooley and Mourne Mountains to the north.

———

Leaving Fourknocks, continue straight along the road, bearing left after 800m and following a sign for Clonalvy; at the next junction, 500m along, turn right. Note the chestnut tree in the middle of the junction, something that was quite common in olden times when the traffic was a lot slower and junctions were important places. Take the right turn in Clonalvy village, following a sign for Ardcath and Kilmoon. After 2.4km (1.5 miles) look out for a circular stone tower on the high ground to the right. This is the remains of a large windmill. More than two centuries ago there were many of these structures in the Fingal area, with their great sails continuously rotating, grinding corn and other cereals.

Continue on across a main road, and go right at Moorpark house—one of the many fine stone-built houses in this area of County Meath. At the next junction go left to reach the busy N2, then turn right, following the sign for Slane. After 4km (2.5 miles) turn left, following the sign for Tara and passing the pretty hamlet of Rathfeigh and Edoxtown (a strange-sounding name, but derived from the name Edock, or Haydock). As you enter the strung-out village of Obertstown, turn right at Swan's Public House and go straight for the village of Skreen, 1.6km (1 mile) further on.

At the top of this tiny village, which is blessed with two pubs, stands St Columba's Church. The key for the tower, which contains an ancient baptismal font and a few fragments of cut stone, can be had from Mrs O'Connell in the pub opposite the church. The hilltop was the location of an early monastery, to which a gold and silver shrine containing the remains of St Columba were brought from England in AD 875. Such relics would have ensured the prosperity of the monastery, but it was raided several times during the tenth, eleventh and twelfth centuries, particularly by the Norse of Dublin, and the holy shrine disappeared into obscurity. From its few surviving cut-stone details it is possible to date the present massive church to the fifteenth century, but its imposing four-storey tower is probably earlier than that. Set into the wall over the south doorway is a sandstone effigy of a bishop that is probably fourteenth century in date. The elevation of the site means the church can be seen from far around and the views from it on a clear day are quite wonderful, seeming even more extensive than those at Tara, nearly 3km (1.8 miles) to the west.

Descending from the church, turn right at Foxes pub and follow a winding road downhill to the N3; take great care, for it is a busy road, and cross straight over and ascend towards Tara. At a T-junction, turn right to reach the car park serving the hilltop monuments and the church, which has been converted into an interpretive centre.

Tara is one of the most famous sites in Ireland, mainly due to the way it was romantically imagined by the poet Thomas Moore and later fantasised in the Gaelic Revival period as the site of the great palace complex of the High Kings of Ireland, which ensured it found its way into the schoolbooks of hundreds of thousands of Irish children during the late nineteenth and most of the twentieth century. In fact, Tara is probably more important and more magical than alluded to in all the glossy imaginings of the Gaelic revival poets.

The grass-covered hill is engraved with the forms of earthen structures that were created at many different times and for many different purposes over a period of more than 4,000 years, including the so-called Mound of the Hostages, which is actually a passage grave dating from 2100 BC, and Rath na Ríogh or the Fort of the Kings, which is a typical, oval Iron Age hillfort. In ancient times Tara was associated with the goddess Maeve, and it clearly continued to be a ceremonial place of great importance for many centuries. All this and much more is described in the audio-visual presentation given in the Tara Interpretive Centre, for which there is a small charge.

Although Tara is not a hugely impressive place visually, it is hard not to be conscious of its long history, evidenced by the grassy mounds and many corrugations that imprint the landscape of the open hill. If you prefer, you can bypass the audiovisuals and interpretations and just wander the open hillside, simply enjoying the air and space and mysterious landforms. Children can enjoy the openness of the place in the simplest way: rolling down the earthen banks.

Beside the car park is a souvenir and bookshop, which stocks lots of books on fairies, witches and Celtic matters, suggesting that Tara has become a bit of a cult centre. There is also a good café where you can get a light lunch.

If you are disappointed by the lack of tangible remains at Tara, where the land formations demand a lot of the imagination, the next site consists of a very definite complex of buildings, albeit in ruinous condition. Leaving Tara, return along the road you came for nearly 1km (0.5 mile), and take a turn to the right. This narrow road winds down the hill to reach a T-junction, where you turn left for Kilmessan. Entering the village, note the parish church to the left. It is a simple building dating from 1731 with a bellcote, but the raised mound on which it stands suggests there has been a church on this site for more than a few centuries.

Turn left and then right out of the village; soon you will pass the Bective Bar, after which you cross the River Boyne and Bective Abbey comes into sight ahead to the right. There is space to park on the left, just after the bridge; the abbey, standing in the middle of a field, is reached by passing through a small, low leaf in a field-gate.

The manor house of Bective consists of a substantial complex of much-altered, stone-built buildings sited a short distance from the River Boyne. It was originally established here in AD 1147 for the Cistercian monks by Murchad O Mclaghlin, the King of Meath, as a daughter house of Mellifont Abbey. The monks reclaimed, developed and farmed well over 4,000 acres here, and the original establishment would have spread in all directions, well beyond the complex you see today, with a harbour on the Boyne for shipping their produce upstream to the Norman stronghold of Trim, or downstream to Slane and Drogheda. In 1196 there was a dispute over where to bury the body of Hugh de Lacy, Norman lord of a huge area of land that extended from County Meath to the River Shannon. Eventually his body was brought here, while his head was buried at St Thomas' Abbey in Dublin. A few years later a judgment was made in favour of St Thomas' and de Lacy's remains were exhumed and taken away to rejoin his head in Dublin.

During the dissolution of the monasteries (1538–1541) the buildings were converted, as was common throughout Ireland and England, into a manor house, with the crude insertion of fireplaces and chimneys and large rectangular windows. While two sides of the cloisters survive as part of the courtyard of the house, the original abbey church has all but disappeared. You can still pick out a number of features of the original buildings, however, including the tall Gothic nave arches in eroded red sandstone, now filled in, and part of a wall.

Retrace your steps to Kilmessan; the Station House Hotel (tel: 046 9025239) has an award-winning restaurant that might be suitable for an evening meal. To return to Dublin, take the road out of Kilmessan towards Dunshaughlin; after 4.8km (almost 3 miles) you will pass by the entrance to Dunsany Castle on the right, and shortly afterwards the sad pile of Killeen Castle can be seen in the distance on the left. Originally a fifteenth-century castle, in more recent times it was the home of the celebrated Elizabeth, Countess of Fingal, who wrote of her life and Dublin society at the turn of the nineteenth/twentieth centuries in *Eighty Years Young*.

At Dunshaughlin take the N3 back to the M50 and Dublin.

Old Gatelodge, Loughcrew

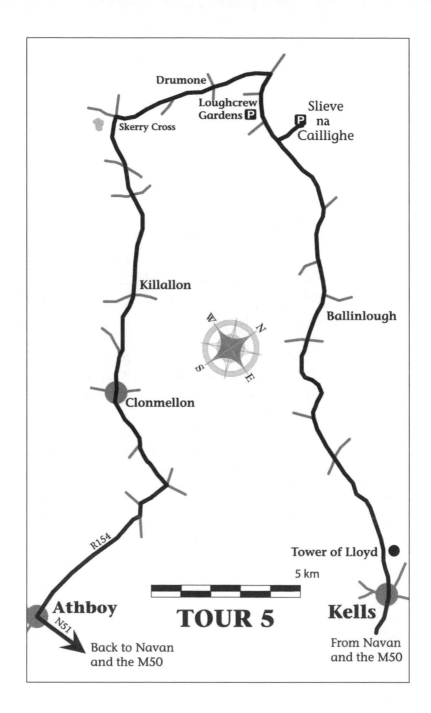

Drumone

Loughcrew
Gardens 🅿

Slieve
na
Caillighe 🅿

Skerry Cross

Killallon

Ballinlough

W N
S E

Clonmellon

R154

Tower of Lloyd ●

5 km

Athboy

TOUR 5

Kells

N51

Back to Navan
and the M50

From Navan
and the M50

Kells, Loughcrew Historic Gardens and the Slieve na Caillighe Neolithic necropolis

ᥱᥴ

This varied tour brings you to the ancient town of Kells, to a restored seventeenth-century pleasure garden and to one of Ireland's most impressive Neolithic sites. Be sure to bring a torch to provide light in the tomb!

ROUTE: Exit 6 from the M50 takes you to Kells via Dunshaughlin and Navan, and side roads take you on to Loughcrew. The return journey is made along quiet country roads via Clonmellon and Athboy to rejoin the outgoing route at Navan.

DISTANCE: 182km (114 miles).

MAPS: OS Discovery numbers 50, 43 and 42.

Leave the M50 at intersection 6 (Navan Road) and follow the N3 to the town of Kells, 54km (33 miles) out, via Dunshaughlin and Navan. Park in front of the Kells Heritage Centre, which is one of the first buildings you meet on the right, on the Dublin side of the town.

Kells is one of the oldest continuously inhabited places in Ireland. Its recorded history begins when the monastery from which it developed was founded in the sixth century by St Columcille, or Columba. Columcille, born about AD 521 in Donegal, was a descendant of the semi-legendary king, Niall of the Nine Hostages, and is perhaps the most famous of the Irish saints after St Patrick. He founded many monasteries in Ireland, but became involved in the earliest recorded example of copyright infringement when he refused to give up a Book of Psalms he had had copied—without permission—from an original owned by St Finian. Laboriously and painstakingly handwritten and handmade by scribes, at the time books were extremely valuable and rare and a transgression such as this was a major matter. The dispute eventually led to a bloody battle in which Columcille's forces triumphed and in which, it is said, 3,000 men were killed. In spite of winning the day and in spite of his position in the Irish Church, Columcille was disgraced and sent into exile with twelve of his monks. They sailed out of Lough Foyle in County Donegal and northwards, eventually establishing the famous monastery on the island of Iona, off the coast of Scotland. Iona became a famed seat of learning and artistry, and it was here that the Book of Kells is said to have been created.

In the ninth century, after repeated and devastating attacks on Iona by the Vikings, the monks fled to Ireland, seeking refuge. There they rejoined the monastery at Kells, which became the leading Columban monastery in Ireland. It was a case of out of the frying pan and into the fire, however: before long the Vikings were attacking and raiding sites in Ireland, and between their expeditions and the attacks launched by local Irish and Norse clans, the monastic city of Kells was sacked and pillaged six times during the tenth century. The Vikings always put profit before mere murder: it is recorded that on one occasion the Dublin Vikings took 3,000 inhabitants of Kells prisoner and sold them into slavery in Iceland and the Near East. Little remains today of the old monastic establishment, but a fine model of the original settlement is displayed in the Heritage Centre and its concentric layout can be traced in the streets of the modern town.

Kells Heritage Centre: entry fee: €4, but with reductions for OAPs and groups. Opening hours: May–September, Monday–Saturday, 10.00am–5.30pm and Sundays and Bank Holidays, 2.00pm–6.00pm; October–April, Monday–Saturday, 10.00am–5.00pm and closed Sundays and Bank Holidays.

The centre is based in a fine old courthouse building that dates from 1801 and was built to the designs of Francis Johnston, who also designed the GPO in Dublin. In front of the centre stands a massive stone High Cross: it used to stand in a narrow street in the middle of the town where it was in danger of being destroyed by a wayward articulated truck, so it was relocated here.

The conversion of the courthouse to a heritage centre was well conceived and well carried out. A history of Kells is shown in an audiovisual theatre, and there is an excellent display of full-size replicas of other Irish High Crosses, medieval decorative metalwork and illuminated manuscripts. Although you will not see the real Book of Kells here, you will see an excellent replica and in my opinion in better conditions than you can in Trinity College, where the original is kept. A sophisticated touch-screen explanation of the illuminated pages of the Book of Kells is also provided which is well worth seeing, particularly as it points out, in the midst of the beauty of the artistry, the errors, the tiny graffiti and the quirky notes made by the scribes.

I recommend that you allow at least an hour in the centre to get the best value out of your visit. The building and displays are wheelchair friendly, and there is a good souvenir and gift shop. The cafeteria serves the usual refreshments, but also does lunches—they must be good because the place is well frequented by locals.

Kells is a small town and can easily be explored on foot from the Heritage Centre. Alternatively, you can drive the couple of hundred metres into the town and park. From the Centre, you pass up Headfort Place, John Street and Market Street to reach the grounds of St Columba's Church of Ireland church of AD 1811. In this area—where there are now but fragments of antiquity—once stood the core of the great monastery of Kells: the great church, the Abbot's House, the Guest House, dormitories, cookhouses, workshops and *scriptorum* and all the other accommodations of a medieval monastic city.

Beside the 'modern' church is a tower, now all that remains of a church erected here in 1578: it is clearly much altered and reconstructed, and is rich in sculptures and inscriptions. Children can hunt for the stone heads depicting Hugh Brady, Archbishop of Meath, Thomas Garvie, Dean of Christchurch, Dublin, and Nicholas Daly, Mayor of Kells in the sixteenth century who oversaw the building of the tower; they can be found over the south door. On the ground around the tower lie fragments of medieval window linings, and nearby are the socketed base of a High Cross and a strange three-legged basin.

There are a couple of High Crosses in the graveyard, which have stood here for 1,200 years. Unlike the modern crosses commonly found in graveyards, the original High Crosses were not erected as memorials to the dead but for the instruction and inspiration of the ordinary people of the time. There is evidence that they were originally painted in bright colours, and one can imagine that when the stone was newly cut and sharp in detail they must have been an amazing sight for an uneducated, illiterate peasantry. The South Cross, near the Round Tower, is perhaps the best preserved, or least damaged, of the Kells crosses and is probably the earliest, dating from the eighth century. A variety of biblical subjects are illustrated on it; see if you can identify the panel showing the miracle of the loaves and the fishes, that showing Adam and Eve with their hands protecting their modesty and Cain striking Abel, or that with four men pulling each other's beards—a strange scene that also appears in the Book of Kells. The East Cross is an unusual one: for some reason lost in time its carved decoration was never finished.

South of the church is a 30m tall, roofless Round Tower or bell-house, and although the internal space must be tiny, it is mentioned in the annals as having served for a few days as the hiding place of Murcadh mac Flainn, grandson of the High King of the time. He had made the mistake of proclaiming himself King of Tara, but there were other, more powerful claimants and he had to flee into the monastery for asylum. On his third night here, as he relaxed in what he thought was a safe place, he was murdered by one of his companions.

To find what is possibly the sole surviving building of the original monastery, leave the churchyard by the main gate and turn left: the terracotta-painted house opposite belongs to Mrs Carpenter, who has the key for Columcille's House, a short distance up the hill. It is a small structure, but massively built in stone, and its survival must be in part because the roof is also constructed in vaulted stone. It was originally located inside the monastic enclosure, but is now divided from the churchyard by a road and stands alone in a grassy plot. The ground level around the building was originally much higher than it is today; the building would have been entered from the west, onto a timber floor over a basement, with a small croft, or attic space, in the roof. Many uses have been attributed to this ancient building, which is thought to date back to at least the eighth century when the Columban monks returned from Iona. The lack of windows of any size and its general robustness suggest it may have been a place of safe and fireproof storage for the books and treasures of the monastery.

———

Return to your car and drive out of Kells; on the west side of the town take the road to the left, signed for Oldcastle. To take in some wonderful views of the countryside around here, turn right less than 2km (1 mile) out of Kells at a sign for the People's Park to reach a car park beside the Tower of Lloyd, one of the finest folly towers in the country. This 30m tall lighthouse-like structure was built in 1791 by the First Earl of Bective in honour of his father, Thomas Taylor, and designed by Henry Baker, a pupil of James Gandon. Apart from its memorial purpose, it was useful as a viewing-point for watching steeplechasing and the hunt, and it was said to have been used as a lookout and signal tower during the Napoleonic Wars. It is no longer possible to climb the tower, but the views from its base, from where it is said you can see five counties, are considerable. To the west are the hills at Loughcrew topped by a large cairn, to the south the Dublin Mountains, while to the north-west the plains of central Ireland stretch all the way towards Donegal. An unusual feature is the plaque where the names of all the principal people involved in the construction of the structure are listed, including the stone-cutter and the head stonemason. Today, the Tower of Lloyd has a very contemporary use: it provides a high and discreet location for a mobile phone transmitter. Nearby is a paupers' grave, where those who died in the Kells Workhouse during the Great Famine are buried, and there is a small Celtic cross marking the place.

———

Return to the main road and continue eastwards. Nearly 4km (2.5 miles) from Kells the high walls of Drumbaragh House are passed on the right. The three-storey mansion was built about 1800 to the designs of Francis Johnston. It was the seat of the Woodward family, and the *cottage orné* lodge of 1839 was designed by nineteenth-century Irish architect, Benjamin Woodward.

After a further 5km (3 miles) take the turn to the right: the road in the opposite direction goes to Crossakeel. Soon the rounded green hills of Loughcrew appear ahead. At Ballinlough you will pass the Gothic schoolhouse and battlemented church of 1829, and after 3km (1.8 miles) turn left at a junction, where Oldcastle is signed to the right. Soon the exquisite little gatelodge of Loughcrew House, a tiny, classical, temple-like building, is passed on the right; the great house stood in a very large demesne to the left, but has burnt down no fewer than three times since its original completion in 1823. What remains today is only a shadow of the original.

A short distance past the gatelodge turn left into a car park signed 'Oliver Plunkett Family Church and Historic Gardens'. Loughcrew Historic Gardens are open from April to October, 12.30pm–5.00pm. Contact them at 049 8541356, or email *info@loughcrew.com*. Entry fee is Û6 per person, with concessions for OAPs, groups and children. It should be noted that access to the ruined church of the Plunkett family is free.

Until the Cromwellian wars of the seventeenth century, a branch of the wealthy Plunkett family owned much of the surrounding countryside here and St Oliver Plunkett, the Archbishop of Armagh who was executed in London in 1681, was born here. By that time the Catholic Plunketts had forfeited their lands and Cromwell's Surgeon General, Sir William Petty, who later organised the first land survey of Ireland, arranged for his son-in-law, William Naper, to take possession of it. He established a residence here in 1673. The Naper family expanded their holdings until, by the end of the eighteenth century, they owned 180,000 acres of fine agricultural land.

The ruined church within a walled graveyard (a spooky place that children will enjoy) can be found down an avenue, past the entrance pavilion and coffee shop. A three-storey residential tower dating from the late fifteenth century, where the priest lived in reasonable security, stands at the west end of the nave. A small chapel, probably built by the Napers, projects from the south wall and in its window has the church's only surviving cut stone, and above the window is an elaborate crest of the Naper family. One of the headstones in the graveyard commemorates Alexander Duggan, stucco plasterer and artist, who died in 1831, and relates how the 'congruous mansion of Loughcrew abounds with many brilliant specimens' of his work.

Loughcrew Gardens, originally laid out in the seventeenth century, are entered through a gate near the church and are dominated by a great motte (a grassy mound of earth) and what remains of the original castle, built here by the Normans at the time of the invasion. Rather than a garden of formal flowerbeds, Loughcrew is a blend of water, trees and follies woven through with historical remains, such as the motte, and the foundations of the original longhouse erected by William Naper in 1673, all set against the beautiful backdrop of the sweeping, grassy Loughcrew hills. There is a fine avenue of gnarled yews, said to date to the seventeenth century, and a set of exquisite nineteenth-century wrought-iron gates set into a limestone classical gateway that is believed to have once framed the entrance to the seventeenth-century longhouse. The garden, filled with sculptures of lurking reptiles, fairies and giant spiders, has many delightful surprises for children.

For those who want to stretch their legs there is a woodland walk that starts to the left of the church and takes you to what remains of Loughcrew House, a sad remnant of the magnificent pillared portico. The round trip of about 4km (2.4 miles) should not take much longer than an hour.

A light lunch of soup, toasted sandwiches and cakes can be enjoyed at the Loughcrew café, where you can also purchase books on Loughcrew and souvenirs and crafts before collecting the key for the Slieve na Caillighe tombs at the desk there and setting off to find them.

Return eastwards along the road for nearly 2km (just over 1 mile) and take a turn left up a side road to a car park.

The Loughcrew Hills present an unusual landscape in Irish terms, in that much of them are without hedges and must resemble what the countryside looked like before enclosures took place in the eighteenth century. Strung along the tops of these two hills is one of Ireland's largest Neolithic cemeteries, consisting of more than thirty individual tombs. Although the larger tombs were built 5,000 years ago, some of the smaller ones are even earlier, and a very large number of the stones and boulders used in the construction of the tombs are richly decorated with Megalithic art.

There are tombs on both hills, so first head up onto the western hill, which has the most cairns—two larger ones and ten smaller—gathered on the plateau-like, hedgeless landscape of rolling green grasslands interspersed with stands of tall trees. It is a truly amazing place and the sheer density of tombs is difficult to credit. The two largest cairns, titled 'L' and 'D', are 133m and 532m in diameter, respectively. Cairn 'D' is massive but, mysteriously, has no passage. You can enter Cairn 'L', however, where at the end of a short passage you reach the burial chamber (this is where you will need your torch). It was repaired some years ago with concrete, but the 'niches' around the passage are as they have been for 5,000 years. In the large niche on the right, behind a pillar, sits a stone basin, which may have been used to contain the ashes of the people buried here. Archaeological excavations turned up some 900 pieces of charred bone and forty-eight human teeth. Looking back along the passage you can see that the nearby hill of Slieve Rua, which used to sport a cairn, is framed by the portals. Nearby, there are two cairns from which the tops have been removed, giving excellent open-plan views of their passages.

The long views from the hilltop are spectacular in clear weather: to the southeast you can identify Three Rock Mountain and Tibradden at the northern end of the Dublin Mountains; the Hill of Allen and its two companions in Kildare are easy to identify, as are the low-lying Slieve Bloom Mountains to the south-west. On the eastern hill the views to the north open up: away beyond the rich green drumlins of Cavan and the glint of Lough Sheelin you can see the Cuilcagh Mountains—gentle slopes to the west and abrupt cliffs on the eastern side. To the north-east you will see Slieve Gullion and the switchback Carlingford Mountains, with the unmistakable shape of Slieve Donard peeking cheekily over the top.

The eastern hill is called Carnbane East, and here you will find six tombs gathered around a larger one that has a passage oriented to receive the rising sun on the annual equinox. The whole hill is striped with lazybeds, the palimpsest of the efforts of local potato farmers a century-and-a-half ago, before the Great Famine.

When you are finished on the Loughcrew Hills, return to your car, drive back downhill and turn right, driving past Loughcrew Gardens again. (Don't forget to hand back the key!) Take the next left turn, which takes you to the hamlet of Drumone. Continue straight through Drumone and at Skerry Cross, a little more than 3km (1.8 miles) from Drumone, turn left. To the south-west, at the crossroads, is the tranquil Lough Ban, which has a crannog, or medieval man-made island dwelling, at its centre, and is picturesquely overlooked by a conical hill.

Keep on straight, following the signs for Clonmellon, passing through the hamlet of Killallon, overlooked by a Norman motte. About 1km (0.5 mile) further on, look out on the right for an unusual sight: a tree, with a riot of colourful rags tied to its branches. In pre-Christian times certain trees were regarded as sacred, a custom that continued into the Christian era, particularly with regard to trees standing near holy wells. Pilgrims would leave offerings on the tree, tying pieces of cloth to the branches to mark their visit, or in hope of having an ailment cured.

At Clonmellon you rejoin the N52 and continue straight through the village, a long, wide market street lined with trees and stone houses. A little more than 1km (0.5 mile) from the village, nineteenth-century Killua Castle can be seen in the distance to the right. I used often visit this great house, which was for many years a picturesque castellated ruin, to admire the limestone facings and decorations that are as sharp as the day they were sculpted and to regret that something could not be done to save it. The demesne is full of whimsical follies and monuments, including a tall obelisk on a nearby drumlin-top, erected by Sir Thomas Chapman in 1810 to commemorate Walter Raleigh's introduction of the potato into Ireland. I was delighted to learn recently that Killua Castle is being comprehensively refurbished.

At the next crossroads turn right onto the R154, heading for Athboy. In Athboy you turn left to follow the N51 to Navan, and thence back to Dublin.

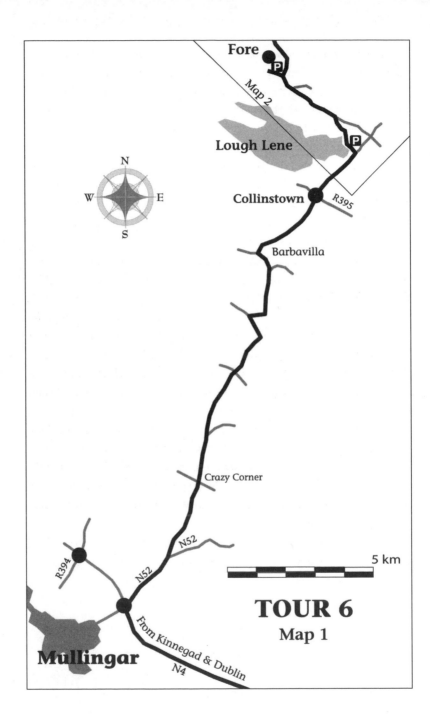

Fore

Map 2

Lough Lene

Collinstown R395

Barbavilla

Crazy Corner

N52

N52

R394

N52

From Kinnegad & Dublin

N4

Mullingar

5 km

TOUR 6
Map 1

Fore Abbey and Mullaghmeen Wood

 දිරි

This tour takes you west to a remote and beautiful fossil landscape of lakes and old limestone hills, to a seventh-century monastery that boasts seven wonders, and on to finish the day with a walk in the largest planted beech forest in Western Europe. You will touch on five counties during the tour.

ROUTE: At about 200km (125 miles), and crossing five counties, this tour is one of the longest in my selection. The N4 and M4 (toll: E2.50) is followed as far as Mullingar, in County Westmeath, and then quiet country roads bring you to Fore and Mullaghmeen. The return journey is made via the towns of Oldcastle and Virginia, to join the N3 at Kells, which takes you back to Dublin.

DISTANCE: 200km (125 miles).

MAPS: OS Discovery numbers 50, 49, 41 and 42.

Take intersection 7 (Lucan exit) from the M50 and drive 77km (48 miles) west for Mullingar, following the N4 and M4 all the way. Turn off the Mullingar bypass, following the signs for the town centre and the N52. At the top of the ramp turn right onto the N52 and head north, in the direction of Delvin. After just under 2km (just over 1 mile) bear left onto a quiet, winding, tree-lined road, passing by places with strange names, such as 'Pass if you can' and 'Crazy Corner'. At the next crossroads go straight through, following the sign for Collinstown. About 7km (4.5 miles) after leaving the Mullingar bypass, look out on the left for a private astronomical observatory attached to a house.

The landscape changes subtly as you progress northwards, slowly becoming a very pretty world of pastures and wood-covered rolling hills. Keep on straight for Collinstown, as the views to each side constantly change. Ten kilometres (6 miles) after leaving the Mullingar by-pass, go right at a Y-junction and shortly after, at a fine stone house, turn right again. The great demesne now on your right is Barbaville, the house of which was built about 1730 by a William Smythe and named after his wife. The pretty village of Collinstown is reached shortly thereafter: go straight through the village, following the sign for Fore.

On your left, after leaving the village, Lough Lean comes into sight; take the first turn left to pass by the shore of this beautiful lake. The lake is picturesquely sited amid wooded hills and is unique in Ireland as its location and height in the flatness of the central plain means that its waters drain both east and west: one outlet stream drains to the River Deal and on to the Boyne and the Irish Sea; the other flows through limestone caverns under the hill to Fore, where it rises in a spring and flows west to the River Inny and on to the River Shannon before reaching the Atlantic Ocean.

Joining the main road again, continue to the left to wind between banks that are covered by rosebay willowherb in late summer, and on into a landscape of steep limestone outcrops. Geologists tell us that two million years ago this was an area of dramatic stone towers and pinnacles standing sentinel over a network of great caves separated by narrow chasms. It was substantially eroded away by glaciation to the soft, rounded hills and valleys you see today, but a few craggy outcrops remain, such as the Ben of Fore over to the right, like ghostly impressions of what was here before.

A little more than 96km (56 miles) from the M50 is the village of Fore. To the right is the modern parish church, completed in the early twentieth century, and behind it lie the scant remains of a pre-Penal chapel and a Lourdes grotto containing a tiny font made from stone brought back from that French shrine. Opposite the church are what remains of the gateway to the medieval monastery of Fore, erected when it was fortified in the mid-fifteenth century. You can see evidence of repairs carried out on the gateway a couple of centuries later in the form of fragments of decorated stone, taken from the original abbey cloister, which are built into the structure. Indeed, much of the village of Fore seems to have been constructed from stone mined at the monastery.

There are two pubs in the tiny village and at one of them, the Seven Wonders pub—a name you would more readily associate with a Chinese takeaway—you can obtain the key for the Anchorite's Cell, more of which later. A little further on is the Fore Visitors' Centre, which has a twenty-minute audio-visual show outlining the history of Fore and a café that serves soups, toasted sandwiches and irresistible cakes. There are also books, guides, maps and home-made jam for sale, and plenty of information about the place; car parking is available around the back.

The monastic buildings of Fore are few minutes' walk further on, scattered over a marshy valley overlooked by a dramatic limestone outcrop, creating an evocative scene. Here St Fechin founded a monastery around AD 610, and within twenty years it had swelled to accommodate 300 monks. Like other monastic centres it attracted the periodic attention of foreign and Irish marauders, and was burnt down twelve times between the eighth and the twelfth centuries. Such efforts notwithstanding, it survived into the Norman period, when it was taken over by the Norman lord of Meath, Hugh de Lacy, who re-established it as a Benedictine foundation in the early thirteenth century. By the mid-fifteenth century it had grown into a monastic town and was an outpost of The Pale, fortified with a town wall, two of the gates of which can still be seen.

The oldest building of the group is St Fechin's Church, sited in a graveyard on the rising ground south of the road. Much added to and altered over the ten centuries of its existence, it has a most impressive trabeated west entrance doorway, with a massive lintel inscribed with a Greek cross. Look out on the left side of the chancel arch for the amusing thirteenth-century carved figure of a seated monk with bulging eyes.

Further up the steep, grassy hill (which children love to roll down) is the nineteenth-century mausoleum of the Greville-Nugent family, erected as an extension to a late medieval tower, which in turn was probably erected to replace a hermit's cell. The key you have collected from the Seven Wonders pub will give access into this strange and spooky place. The last hermit to occupy the tower was Patrick Beglen in the early seventeenth century. He was one of Ireland's last anchorites, and lived in such incredibly cramped circumstances that he became known as 'The Holy Man in the Stone'.

North of the road lie the main monastic buildings: the much-altered Abbey of St Taurin and St Fechin (the name Taurin comes from the Abbey of St Taurin in Normandy, which was the mother house of Fore). It is clearly a fortified establishment, and can be reached only by a convoluted pathway across the marsh, which must have helped in its defence. Beside the path leading to the abbey are the ruins of an old mill that was in use until 1875, which took water from an underground river to drive its wheel. The river flows from Lough Lene, over the hill to the south. The mill is called the Mill Without the Race and is one of the Seven Wonders of Fore, said to have appeared miraculously when summoned by St Fechin. A little further along you will find a phenomenon that was once common in Ireland but is now rarely seen. Over a heap of chaotic stone slabs, called St Fechin's Bath, stand the gnarled remains of a sacred tree, festooned with all kinds of rags, strips of colourful cloth, children's socks and handkerchiefs, and with numerous coins hammered into its bark. The waters of the 'bath' are supposed to be therapeutic for children's ailments, and the rags are left by people hoping for a cure—a custom that surely harks back to pre-Christian, pagan times.

Most of the abbey's buildings, including the cloisters, were repaired and reconstructed during the twentieth century from fragments scattered around the site. There are a few sculptural stones built into the walls; children will have fun searching for the saint's head, which can be found between two loop windows on the face of a tower that projects from the east side of the complex. Medieval buildings were always much altered during the few hundred years they were occupied, and you can often trace those changes because medieval builders didn't bother covering up what existed before, so you can see the lines of different roofs that originally ended at the towers, and on the west side look out for the ghost of an old doorway in the masonry.

At the back of the monastic buildings, up a flight of steps, are the remains of a dovecote, complete with nesting niches. In the Middle

Ages, upwards of 1,000 pigeons were reared and kept for the table; month-old pigeon chicks were a particular delicacy. Pigeons' eggs were also enjoyed, while their feathers were used in bedding and their guano was used to augment the lime fertiliser on the fields.

Inside the church, plastered sections of walls still retain vestiges of the original painted decoration, depicting in faded colour coursed masonry with a red rosette in the centre of each brick.

St Fechin's Well can be found near the car park. An old sacred tree once stood over it, of which only a stump remains, although a new one has been planted to take its place. The new one is already over-burdened with rags, while the old stump is shiny with hammered-in coins. The old tree is said to have only ever grown three branches in honour of the Blessed Trinity, and the water from the well, now dried up for much of the year, was said to be impossible to boil. These anomalies are listed as two more of the Seven Wonders of Fore.

The whole place has a great feeling of tranquillity, particularly when there are few visitors around, and sitting on the grassy hill above the Anchorite's Cell you can feel centuries away from Dublin City.

To leave Fore for Mullaghmeen Wood, go back through the village and turn left. Turn left at the next T-junction and shortly after, with due care, take a right turn off the main road as it bears sharply to the left. At the next junction, just over 4.5km (2.7 miles) from Fore, bear left onto a side road and shortly after the rounded Hill of Moat will hove into view. At almost 7.5km (4.5 miles) from Fore, turn right at a crossroads, following a sign for 'Mullaghmeen Country'. The gateway to Mullaghmeen Wood is a little over 1.5km (1 mile) away; drive in and park in the woodland car park.

Mullaghmeen Wood covers 1,000 acres on the borders of counties Meath and Westmeath, on lands purchased by the Department of Agriculture in the early 1930s. Consisting of old fields, copses and a laurel wood at the eastern side, soil tests in the area confirmed that the brown earth over limestone was ideal for the growth of a deciduous forest and a planting project was put in place, providing welcome

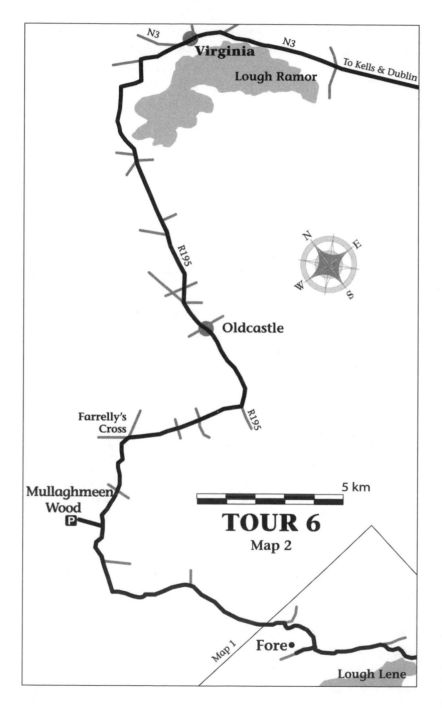

N3

Virginia

N3

To Kells & Dublin

Lough Ramor

R195

Oldcastle

N
E
W
S

R195

Farrelly's
Cross

Mullaghmeen
Wood
P

5 km

TOUR 6

Map 2

Map 1

Fore•

Lough Lene

employment in those hard times to upwards of 120 men. The laurel wood posed a problem because laurels spread rapidly, like rhododendrons, and prevent other species from flourishing. Someone came up with the bright idea that they would make good raw material in the manufacture of charcoal, and for some years this process was successfully carried out. The common beech, native to Europe from Scandinavia to Bulgaria and one of the most stately and beautiful of forest trees, was chosen as the main species at Mullaghmeen. The beech didn't make it to Ireland after the retreat of the ice, but was imported in the late seventeenth and early eighteenth century by estate-owners developing commercial forestry: it was a widely used timber and it still is a valuable material for furniture-making. Here at Mullaghmeen, its early pale green filmy leaves create a wonderful light in the forest in early summer, contrasting with the russet forest floor, while the golden hues of its autumn foliage make a particularly beautiful contribution to the landscape. Today the forest has also been planted with larch, ash, sitka spruce and noble fir.

Due to the lack of outlook—it is a real Sherwood Forest-type wood and in few places, other than on the perimeter, can you see out to the wider landscape—Mullaghmeen is regularly used for orienteering; the National Orienteering Championships were held there in 2001. At weekends it is a popular place for walkers and many families make use of it. It is home to badgers and foxes and to the grey squirrel, the first examples of which were released not far away, at Castleforbes, in 1911, and you may also glimpse the colourful blue jay or pheasants, which are particularly tame when the shooting season is not in swing.

There is a hierarchy of trails through and around the wood, including what is called the Golden Mile, which is truly golden with leaves in autumn, and they are clearly marked with red or white markers making it difficult to ever lose the way. In the northern end of the wood is White Hill, at 261m above sea level the highest point in County Westmeath. It is not on either the red or white trails, but with careful examination of the map of the wood at the car park, you should be able to find it. It is less than 2km (little more than 1 mile) from the car park as the crow flies and should not take much more than thirty minutes to locate. A small ruined cairn marks the highest point on the hill, from where a gap in the trees gives a marvellous glimpse of Lough Sheelin.

———

Driving out of Mullaghmeen Wood, turn left to pass out of Westmeath and into Meath, and about 3km (1.8 miles) from the wood turn right at Farrelly's Crossroads. Keep on straight, meeting the R195 just over 4km (2.5 miles) further on, then turn left to reach the town of Oldcastle. On the way into town look out for the Gilson Endowed School, a tall structure on the right built in 1823 by Laurence Gilson, a native of Oldcastle who made good in London.

If you had a snack at the visitors' centre at Fore and enjoyed a walk at Mullaghmeen, you should now have a good appetite for a more substantial 'high tea', which you can get in the square of Oldcastle, either at the Naper Arms, the local hotel, or at Gibney's pub, a stone-faced Georgian building that has a café-bar interior and was full of family groups when I visited. I really like the centre of Oldcastle: it is a pleasant place, a triangular 'square' of good Georgian and Victorian houses and shops. Gibney's shop, just across from the pub, has a fine decorative stucco façade that dates from 1862. Just off the square is an antique shop with a Victorian brick-and-terracotta façade: it has a wonderfully chaotic display of stock, where you feel you are sure to find a bargain.

Leave Oldcastle by the road to Virginia, and after about 4km (2.5 miles) you enter County Cavan, the fifth county of the day. Soon you will catch glimpses of Lough Ramor to the right before you reach a T-junction and turn right for the town of Virginia, named, like the American state, after Elizabeth, the 'virgin queen'. Thomas Sheridan, who lived nearby, was the grandfather of the playwright Richard Brinsley Sheridan, and was frequently visited by Jonathan Swift, who wrote much of *Gulliver's Travels* here. A large suburbia of new houses has grown up on the outskirts of this little market town, an eastern outpost of a long county that stretches over 80km (50 miles) towards the north-west coast. The Park Hotel, situated in its own landscaped grounds on the right as you enter town, is a good place for food. The Lakeside Manor Hotel, a short distance from the east side of the town, overlooks the extensive Lough Ramor.

At Virginia you join the N3 and head east for Kells, Navan and Dublin, joining the M50 at intersection 6.

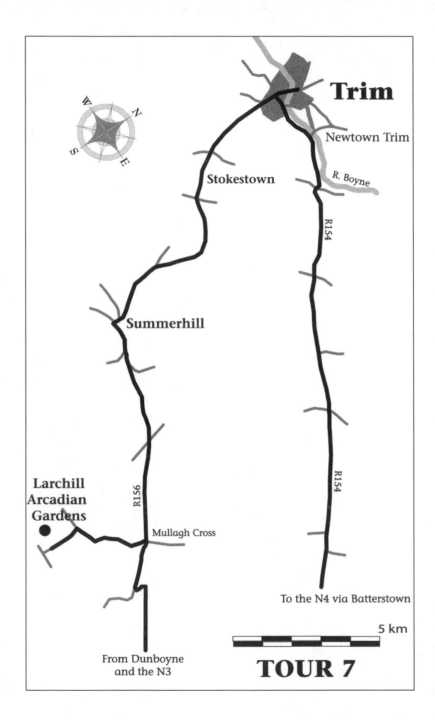

Trim

Newtown Trim

R. Boyne

Stokestown

R154

Summerhill

Larchill
Arcadian
Gardens

R156

Mullagh Cross

R154

To the N4 via Batterstown

From Dunboyne
and the N3

5 km

TOUR 7

Larchill Arcadian Gardens, Trim, its Castle and environs

ℓℓ

Larchill Arcadian Gardens represent a unique survivor from gardening history combined with a farmland wonderland for children. The County Meath town of Trim was once an important centre, evidenced by the rich collection of medieval buildings in its environs, the most dramatic of which is the largest and finest castle in Ireland, Trim Castle, often called King John's Castle.

ROUTE: The N3 and R156 are followed to Clonee, Dunboyne and Summerhill, taking a brief detour to Larchill Gardens on the way. From Summerhill the R158 is taken to Trim, and the return journey is made via Batterstown and the N3.

DISTANCE: 85km (53 miles).

MAPS: OS Discovery numbers 50, 49 and mainly 42.

Exit the M50 at intersection 6 (N3, Navan and Cavan road), and less than 6.5km (4 miles) from the M50 go left off the dual carriageway and through a roundabout onto the R156, heading for Clonee. You enter County Meath before passing through the scattered village of Clonee and continuing on the R156, following signs for Dunboyne. After passing through the village of Dunboyne you are truly out into the plains of Meath, and the roadside is lined with stud farms and prosperous-looking bungalows mingled with traditional labourers' cottages. A good family game for this road is to try to categorise the many different styles of bungalow, inventing names for them, such as 'Georgiana', or 'Rustica', and count how many of each type you pass on the way.

About 11km (7 miles) from Dunboyne is Mullagh Crossroads. Turn left onto the R125 and after nearly 3km (1.8 miles) look out for Larchill Arcadian Gardens on the right: there is plenty of parking on-site. Pre-booked groups and school tours are welcome, with ample car- and coach-parking available. Larchill is open June–August, Tuesday–Sunday and Bank Holiday Weekends, 12 noon–6.00pm; May, Bank Holiday Weekends, September, open weekends only. Entrance fee: adults €7.50; children €5.50; family (two adults and four children) €27.50. Family season tickets are also available, and Larchill has limited disabled access. (website: *www.larchill.ie*).

Larchill is a unique survivor of a type of eighteenth-century garden called a *ferme ornée,* incorporating a trend away from the formal garden and towards natural landscape, a move partly influenced by the philosophies of the early Romantic movement. Into this landscape follies, mock cottages, ruins and picturesque walks were introduced: indeed, peasants—the more bucolic, the better—were often paid to live briefly in the mock cottages so they could be seen through the windows by the ladies and gentlemen of the aristocracy as they perambulated through the garden, as if they were real pedestrians walking through open countryside. Such a garden was created at Versailles by Marie Antoinette, and she used to dress up as a milk-maid to complete the picture.

The *ferme ornée* at Larchill was a lost garden for many years until the de Las Casas family bought the place in the early 1990s and discovered its ten follies, overgrown but reclaimable. They set about restoring the eighteenth-century landscape with assistance from The Great Gardens of Ireland Restoration Programme and FÁS, resulting in the gardens you see today, and they have received many awards for their efforts, including the 2002 Europa Nostra Award for Cultural Heritage—the first time an Irish site received this prestigious prize.

The gardens slope down towards the south-east and are set against a backdrop of the Dublin-Wicklow Mountains. One of the major features is a small, man-made lake complete with islands. The lake was filled in when the de Las Casas arrived: the previous owner had received a grant to fill it in, and the de Las Casas had to apply for a grant to restore it! The largest island on the lake is an elaborate, but miniature pentagonal fort called Gibraltar, which it seems was used in the eighteenth century as the centrepiece of mock sea-battles.

An informal rustic walk takes you down from the farm buildings and around the lake, past some of the follies and the exotic livestock that the de Las Casas keep, in line with the usual eighteenth-century practice when strange animals would have been brought back from the Grand Tour and displayed. The surroundings are like an exciting 'outback' for children, with herds of tiny Soay sheep from the Hebrides roaming about and here and there a llama or an emu, or huge but docile Highland cattle with enormous horns.

One of the follies you pass on the walk, a shallow mound topped by a rustic temple, is called The Foxes' Earth. It is a mausoleum built by the creator of the *ferme ornée*, Robert Watson, who was convinced he would be reincarnated as a fox because he had been instrumental in hunting and killing so many of them during his lifetime. In the mound under the temple he constructed a clever refuge for a fox, organised so that a fox could enter but hounds could not, so that if he were chased in his afterlife, he would have a safe haven! He also banned fox-hunting on his land.

The walled garden at Larchill is a pretty place where exotic vegetables and flowers are grown. In the corner stands a three-storey tower, the rooms of which are decorated with seashells, a common decorative pastime of the ladies of leisure in the eighteenth century.

Apart from the historic and scenic aspects of Larchill, there is lots for children to see and enjoy, particularly the animals. Apart from the Soay sheep and llamas, there is a pets' corner with ducks, geese, goats, guinea pigs and monstrous, incredibly ugly, but friendly rare-breed pigs. Snacks are provided in the tea-rooms, and there is a sandpit for toddlers and a vast two-acre playground for older children.

In addition, Larchill put on a variety of family activities and entertainment events, such as archery classes, falconry, Punch and Judy shows and art workshops: check the website to see what's on when you are visiting. These attractions, and many others, make a visit to Larchill a must.

Return the way you came from Mullagh Crossroads and turn left. Soon after, you enter the village of Summerhill. The robust limestone gates to the great house of same name are on the left, opposite the village green. Built about 1731, it was probably the most dramatic of the great Irish Palladian houses, but like so many others it was lost to the nation when it was burnt down by republicans in 1922, during the War of Independence. It remained a magnificent ruin until 1957, when it was demolished. On the pleasant village green, around which some of the original houses of the late eighteenth-century village survive, is the shaft of a sixteenth-century stone cross with richly carved ornament: note, in particular, the hunting scene running up the east side, complete with stag and hounds. It is good to remember that these village greens, usually landscaped today like a little park, were in the past important commercial spaces where fairs were held, providing an opportunity for local people to sell or trade their wares and produce. Fairs could be held only by the grant of the king, and in the case of Summerhill the village was permitted to hold four fairs each year, in April, June, September and November.

Turn right at the green and follow the R158 towards Trim. The road climbs a low hill at Stokestown, giving long views across the lands of Meath to the south and west, before descending to reach the town of Trim. Drive into the centre, past the statue of the Duke of Wellington atop a tall Corinthian column; as a young man he lived in Trim while he was secretary to Trim Corporation, and this monument was erected in his honour by the landowners of Meath in 1817, not long after his defeat of Napoleon at Waterloo. Parking should not be too difficult to find, and there is a public car park beside the Castle.

Trim is a small town, full of interesting and historical buildings and easily navigated on foot. Begin your exploration with a visit to the Tourist Office, near the entrance to the castle, where you can get a simple map of the town. (Tourist Office: open 10.00am–5.00pm, Monday–Wednesday; closed Thursdays; open 10.00am–6.00pm Fridays; 10.00am–5.00pm Saturdays; 12.00–5.00pm Sundays.) The Meath Heritage and Genealogical Centre occupies the floor over the Tourist Office.

Although partially ruined, the castle of Trim is the largest and one of the best preserved Anglo-Norman castles in Ireland. The outer defence walls enclose over three acres of land, and the keep, with square towers on three of its sides, has a footprint of over 4,000 square feet. It was built in the early thirteenth century on the site of an earlier structure erected by the Norman knight Hugh de Lacy in 1174, just five years after the commencement of the Norman Conquest.

Access to the three acres of the grounds of the castle, within the outer walls, is €1.50. Entry to the three floors of the great 25m tall stone-built keep is €3.50.

In the 800 years it has occupied this site the castle has been witness to many historical events. Geoffrey de Geneville, who extended the castle in the later thirteenth century, was a Crusader who fought against the Saracens in the Holy Land for three years, and on his return was appointed Lord Justice of Ireland by his friend, King Edward I. For a century or two after, Trim was one of the most important towns in Ireland and the Irish Parliament sat in the castle on many occasions. Henry of Lancaster, who would later become King Henry V, was a prisoner in the castle for a while on the orders of King Richard II. Silken Thomas would have spent time here when his forces captured Trim in 1536, and a little more than a century later, in 1647, the castle and the town were damaged by cannonfire when they were taken by the Confederate army. Two years later the castle suffered considerable destruction when it was besieged and captured by the Cromwellian forces.

The keep was designed with a cruciform plan so that no matter from which quarter it was approached, the 'visitor' was in the line of fire from some part of the battlements. The walls are 4m thick and the stairs and passages serving the upper floors are 'intermural', meaning they are built within the thickness of the walls. It is altogether an impressive piece of medieval construction, and well worth visiting. The castle was an important location for the movie, *Braveheart*.

After your visit to the castle, cross the River Boyne by the modern timber footbridge; looking north you can see the four Gothic arches of the town bridge, which dates from the 1390s and is perhaps the oldest surviving unaltered bridge in Ireland. Ascend the grassy slope to the Yellow Steeple, a spectacularly high ruin of a seven-storey tower built in the late fourteenth century. Reaching nearly 40m above the Boyne, it was attached to St Mary's Abbey and was partially destroyed during the Cromwellian siege of Trim. The Abbey housed a statue of Our Lady that was said to have miraculous powers and which attracted great numbers of pilgrims to Trim: indeed, the pilgrims' financial offerings supported the Abbey. So impressed was King Henry IV by the statue that he signed an Act of Parliament giving protection to pilgrims to Trim, including those that might be 'Irish rebels', to whom he gave immunity from arrest on any charge.

Beside the tower stand the much-altered fourteenth-century buildings of the Abbey, with their Elizabethan gables facing over the river. These buildings have a multifaceted history. Although the Abbey was suppressed by Henry VIII, the buildings were briefly considered as a site for the establishment of an Irish university. When the university was eventually established at Trinity College in Dublin, Elizabeth I founded a Latin School in the Abbey. In the early eighteenth century the school was owned for a time by Dean Swift, and eventually counted among its students the young Duke of Wellington and the mathematician Sir Rowan Hamilton. Hamilton was very interested in astronomy (he was appointed Astronomer Royal of Ireland at the tender age of twenty-two), and it is said he used to observe the stars from the little iron balcony still to be seen on the north gable of the building.

Also worth visiting in the town is St Patrick's Church of Ireland Cathedral. It is often locked, so it is worthwhile enquiring at the Tourist Office about gaining entrance. It is said to be built on the site of a church founded by St Patrick and, with the exception of the fifteenth-century tower, it dates from the twelfth century, although it has been much altered and reconstructed. Of particular interest are the many decorated tombstones mounted in the walls, some dating back to the sixteenth century.

If you are not going to have a picnic by the Boyne, there are plenty of eating-places in the town. There are two good cafés in Market Street, which has been in existence since it was established by the Normans, when cattle, pigs and poultry were sold; wool and hardware were sold in the Market Yard beside the Town Hall. There are also a couple of restaurants, and a chip shop overlooking the car park beside the castle.

I can highly recommend a walk along the Boyne to the extensive remains of an old settlement known as Newtown Trim, where a satellite town to Trim was planned in the fourteenth century, but later abandoned. The walk, returning by road, should take about an hour.

Cross the footbridge opposite the castle again and turn right along the river path, passing the Sheep's Gate, one of the old town gates. A good impression of the extent of Trim Castle can be had by looking back from the road-bridge. Follow the path under the road-bridge and cross a stile onto a well-frequented grassy anglers' path. It is a pleasant stretch of the Boyne, often cruised by swans and geese, and makes a peaceful contrast to the busy town. Before long the tall gables of the ruined Cathedral of SS Peter and Paul come into view around a bend of the river. Adjoining the cathedral and between it and the river stand the ruins of the Victorine Abbey, founded by the Norman knight Simon de Rochfort about 1206; he is buried under the Abbey's high altar.

Walk up through the field to enter the ruins, now surrounded by a graveyard that is still in use. At the eastern end of the graveyard is the old parish church, which probably pre-dates the cathedral and abbey. Within it is the sixteenth-century carved limestone tomb of Sir Lucas Dillon and his wife, Lady Jane Bathe; their lichen-speckled recumbent effigies in the dress of the period lie on the top. It is known locally as 'the tomb of the man and jealous woman', perhaps referring to the fact that after his wife's death, Sir Lucas married again but is buried with his first wife.

Leaving the graveyard, cross the nearby medieval bridge to reach the ruin of yet another ancient establishment, the Priory of St John the Baptist, founded in the early thirteenth century for the Crossed Friars, so-called for the cross they wore on the front of their habits. The order was originally founded to assist the Christian armies with medical care during the Crusades to the Holy Land. Besides a keep, a chapel and the remains of a bawn tower, there are many compartments, doorways and passages scattered around the site that would do well for a children's game of chase or hide-and-seek.

Return across the bridge, and if you are not going to stop for refreshments at the tiny pub beside the bridge (called David's Lad, after a famous horse), you can return a little more than 1km (0.75 mile) to Trim along the roadside footpath, which takes you into High Street via Navan Gate Street.

Return to Dublin via the R154 and Batterstown; the outgoing route (the N3) is joined near Clonee and the M50 is reached in about 35km (22 miles).

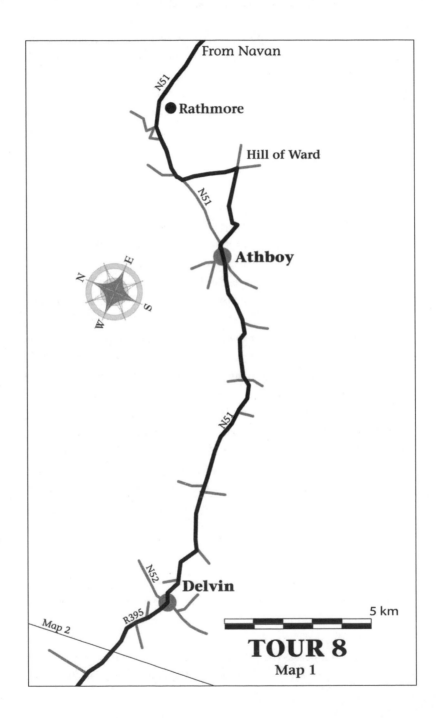

TOUR 8

North-west Meath and Tullynally Castle and Gardens

ℰℰ

Ｎorth-west Meath and eastern Westmeath are rich in fine villages and well-preserved medieval sites. While this is one of the longest tours, I could not resist including some of these along the way, so it is best covered on a long summer's day. Tullynally Castle, the home of the Pakenham family for nearly 400 years and one of the most romantic castles in Ireland, is set in a beautiful demesne of woods and lakes.

ROUTE: **The N3, N51 and R395 are followed via Navan, Athboy and Delvin to Castlepollard and Tullynally. The return journey is via the R394 to meet the N4 at Mullingar, and thence to Dublin, via the M4 (toll: E2.50).**

DISTANCE: **225km (140 miles).**

MAPS: **OS Discovery numbers 50, 49 and mainly 42 and 41.**

Leave the M50 at intersection 6 and drive to Navan. Immediately after entering the outskirts of the town and passing under the arched railway viaduct, take the turn left uphill to a roundabout. Go right, following the sign for Athboy, and take the left at the next traffic lights. Go right at a Y-junction just after the Tailteann Stadium: Athboy is now 19km (11.8 miles) away. Nearly 12km (7.5 miles) outside Navan, look out for a sign indicating you are entering Rathmore. You will pass the primary school, then 700m further on you will see the ruined Rathmore Church in to the left, across a field. There is space for a car to park beside the gate, from where a faint track leads across the field to the church.

Rathmore Church was dedicated to St Laurence and built in the fifteenth century by the Plunketts, who owned large areas of land in the midlands and the east. It is a typical 'wild west' church of the period. At the time, the Anglo-Irish outside The Pale were subject to frequent disturbances and attacks by the Gaelic clans, who often had been the original owners of the lands the Anglo-Irish now occupied. It is easy to see that, with its battlemented parapets and cross-bow loops in the walls, this is a fortified building, designed for easy defence in the times before gunpowder was widely used.

The building is a treasure house of stone carvings: there are lots of bits and pieces of another age to be discovered. The shaft of a baptismal font stands inside the door, with easily discernible representations of New Testament scenes carved in each of its eight sides, including the baptism of Christ and SS Peter and Paul. Inside the vaulted sacristy is the tomb of Thomas Plunkett and his wife, Marion Cruise, with their effigies on top: hers is badly damaged, but his shows clearly the formal apparel of a knight of the time—a tunic of chainmail with bosses at the shoulder and elbows, a dagger on his belt and his armoured feet rest on a faithful dog. A staircase leads up to the priest's apartment above the sacristy—fun for children to explore—and a further stair leads up to where a second floor, now gone, used to be. To the right of the altar is a neat stone *piscine*, or washbasin, complete with plughole.

The east window has some of the earliest carved Gothic tracery in County Meath: the Plunketts were a cosmopolitan and well-travelled lot, and just like travellers of today they enthusiastically brought back all the latest ideas and styles to their rural domains.

On the north wall is a mysterious and rare carved depiction of a labyrinth. A labyrinth is a maze-like series of passages in, or under a building, the most famous being that at Knossos on the island of Crete where the Minotaur prowled. Such artefacts as this probably date from the early Norman period, and have connections with the elusive Holy Grail and pilgrimage to Jerusalem.

The tower originally had a timber stair, and the roof is of corbelled construction. Another stair would have led up to a timber rood loft in the church, where the Plunketts would have been able to worship without having to rub shoulders with their tenants.

As you return to the car, the ruins of the castle the Plunketts lived in can be seen over on the right, nestled in a grove of trees.

Continue on until you reach a T-junction and take the left turn signed for Delvin and Athboy. After a couple of hundred metres take a quiet side road to the left, which brings you up onto the Hill of Ward, from where, if the leaves are off the trees, you will get fine views of the surrounding countryside. In ancient times this hill, called Tlachta, was an important place of annual assembly at the beginning of winter (*Samhain*), an assembly that it is said all the men of Ireland attended. It must have been a busy place! In the seventeenth century Cromwell's army made an encampment here.

Turn right at the crossroads on the hill and descend into Athboy, turning left up the main street. In medieval times Athboy was one of the four walled towns of County Meath and an important market centre. It has a nicely curved main street and is a pleasant place to wander around. The Church of Ireland church, set back from the main street, is worth a visit. Part of the medieval walls of the town can be found bordering the graveyard. The building represents 500 years of construction: the massive tower is fifteenth century, the adjoining building is seventeenth century and the cruciform chapel is nineteenth century. Children can compete in searching for a grotesque head set in the wall as a talisman to drive away the devil: look for it high up on the east wall.

Head west out of the town, bearing right for Delvin. Less than 6km (3.6 miles) further on, as you pass a ruined late medieval towerhouse with a circular corner tower, you leave County Meath and enter County Westmeath.

The village of Delvin is dominated by the remains of a great castle that originally had four corner towers; today only two remain, but it is still an impressive sight. Early in the Norman Conquest, Henry II granted Hugh de Lacy a huge area of land that extended from County Meath to the River Shannon. De Lacy's only problem was that The O'Rourke, the Gaelic Lord of Meath and whose family had been there for centuries, believed he still owned the land. The Normans were nothing if not pragmatic: de Lacy arranged a meeting with O'Rourke, during which he killed him, thus resolving the situation most definitely! He then carved up the region between his own followers. Gilbert de Nugent, his son-in-law, got the land around Athboy, and the castle was built during the thirteenth century. As evidence that those violent times are not really so long ago, the Nugents are still here in Athboy, living in Clonyn Castle to the west of the town.

Near the castle is the ruined church. Note how the Gothic doorway was inserted into an older façade, unselfconsiously leaving the traces of the previous door or window above it.

At the north end of the village, set in terraced lawns, is the neo-Gothic Church of the Assumption, built in 1873 and described as one of the most picturesque churches in Leinster.

Take the road beside the church out of the village, on the left passing the gates to Clonyn Castle and the Delvin Golf Club. Nearly 10km (6 miles) from Delvin the road descends into Collinstown village with its pleasant little market place. A short distance out of the village, Lough Lene can be glimpsed down to the right, embowered in forested hills. After a considerable extent of flat midlands you enter a contrasting drumlin country, characterised by pleasantly rolling hills.

About 7km (4.2 miles) from Collinstown you enter the village of Castlepollard, one of the prettiest villages in the province of Leinster, with its informal market square overlooked by the clock tower and spire of the parish church, and surrounded by an assembly of comfortable late Georgian houses and a few shops and pubs. The church dates to 1827 but, like the rest of the village, it is clear the financial support of the local landowners—the Earls of Longford, to the west, and the Pollards, to the south—was not wanting. It has a simple, austere, but warm interior and I particularly like the swirling staircase up to the organ loft that is the feature of the porch.

If you have arrived in time for lunch, the Pollard Arms hotel is a good bet, serving good, well-cooked plain food.

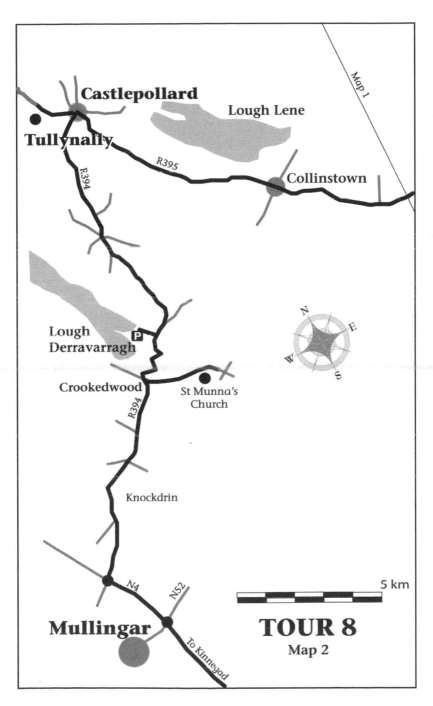

Castlepollard

Lough Lene

Tullynally

R395

Collinstown

R394

Lough
Derravarragh

P

Crookedwood

St Munna's
Church

R394

N

E

W

S

Knockdrin

5 km

N4

N52

Mullingar

To Kinnegad

TOUR 8
Map 2

Map 1

For Tullynally, passing the Pollard Arms on your left, take the first left turn: the entrance gates are about 1km (0.5 mile) out of the village.

Tullynally probably dates back to the sixteenth century, but it came into the ownership of Henry Pakenham in 1655 at the end of the long and bitter wars that culminated in the Cromwellian conquest. Pakenham had been a captain of a troop of horse in the wars and, as happened for many of the soldiers on the winning side, land was his payment and he got Tullynally. The Pakenhams have lived here now for ten generations, and with 120 rooms and a footprint of two acres it is the largest castle in Ireland that is still a private dwelling. The place has been altered and extended many times over the years, involving architects of the stature of Francis Johnston, James Sheil and Sir Richard Morrison.

The Pakenhams were raised to the peerage in 1756 as the Barons of Longford; as a young officer the Duke of Wellington married Kitty Pakenham, one of the daughters of the house, in spite of the fact that her father told him he was not good enough for her. The Pakenhams were and are a colourful family; the Second Earl was the sworn enemy of Daniel O'Connell and Catholic Emancipation, while his son became a Catholic and a monk and founded the Irish Passionist order at Mount Argus in Dublin. The Sixth Earl served as an Irish Senator and devoted his life to the theatre and wrote many books, including the official biography of Éamon de Valera. The current Earl is also an author, of books on Africa, the Boer War and the 1798 Rebellion.

The grounds of Tullynally Castle were first laid out in the eighteenth century as a formal water garden with cascades, fountains and canals, but this layout eventually gave way to the later fashion for naturalistic pleasure grounds: the extensive parklands have been improved, extended and added-to ever since. From the castle terraces, which date from Victorian times, you pass into the informal woodland where you will find many exotic species of trees, some of which were planted more than 200 years ago. Another path leads towards the walled flower garden, and on the way there is a fine view of Knockeyon, the conical hill that overlooks Lough Derravarragh. A ferny path takes you to a grotto that dates back to the original formal gardens, and from which there is a view of Derravarragh, a magical lake that is mentioned in the legend of the Children of Lir.

The Kitchen Garden is one of the largest in Ireland and assisting the gardeners in keeping the grass down are the farm calves and a pair of llamas.

The woodland gardens are quite extensive and to explore them properly you need to have suitable, rugged footwear.

———

The return to Dublin is via the N4, which is reached north of Mullingar. On the way there, two places are well worth visiting: Lough Derravarragh and St Munna's Church.

Return to Castlepollard and take the Mullingar road (R394) out of the village. It is a most scenic route, with the road weaving between and up and down fine grassy hills of large fields, scattered with grazing sheep and parkland oak trees. Just over 8km (4.8 miles) out of Castlepollard, look out for a sign for Lough Derravarragh and turn right onto a narrow road leading down to the lake. You can park close to the water's edge. This southern extremity of the 9.5km (5.8 miles) long, narrow lake is a wonderfully peaceful and evocative place, hemmed in on both sides by tall, wooded hills, the one on the right being Knockeyon, last viewed from the grounds of Tullynally Castle. When I visited there was no one else about and I was delighted to see four swans far out on the waters. Legends tell of the four children of Lir, changed by a jealous stepmother into swans for 900 years, the first 300 of which they had to spend here at Lough Derravarragh. They retained their human senses and were gifted with beautiful singing voices, and the strange, unearthly quality of the music they made brought joy to those who heard it. After 900 years, and with the arrival of Christianity to pagan Ireland, they turned back into humans and were baptised by St Mochaomhog before they died at a very great age.

Rejoin the R394 and continue south; less than 2km (just over 1 mile) after leaving the lake you reach Crookedwood. Turn left onto a side road opposite The Wood public house and follow it for just over 1.5km (1 mile). When you come to a length of high stone wall on the left, look out for St Munna's Church, which is on the right and set back from the road. There is space to park a car at the entrance gate. St Fintan, or

Sheela-na-gig over window at St Munna's Church

Munna, founded a monastery here in the sixth century, but, like Rathmore church, St Munna's is a fortified building with priests' quarters in the tower, dating from about the fifteenth century, and a stone vaulted roof that is almost fully intact: a rare survival against the odds. The key to the church used to be available from the bungalow across the road, but there was no one there when I called. It is not essential to get in, however: most of the interior, which is bare, can be viewed through the east window. Apart from its wonderful intactness and picturesque setting, there are lots of details to find and admire. One can make out that the window surrounds, although not complete, would originally have been very decorative. There is a fine sheela-na-gig over one of the windows—sufficiently eroded to protect modesty—a bishop's head over the door and another head high on the west gable. A point to note: this church is not shown on the second edition of the OS Discovery map.

Across the road, behind a great walled enclosure, are the remains of a small tower marked 'castle' on the OS map.

On the top of the hill to the south-south-east of the church is a fine, little-disturbed motte with an outer earthen ring. The view from the motte is magnificent; ask at award-winning Crookedwood House Restaurant and Guest House, a few hundred metres further uphill from the church, about permission to walk across to visit it.

Return to the R394 and continue south, soon passing the imposing castellated gates of Knockdrin Castle, a romantic mansion designed by James Sheil and built about 1810. Opposite the gates is the Belfry Restaurant and cookery school, housed in a former Church of Ireland church, which was unroofed in 1987 but has been beautifully rescued for its new purpose.

Nearly 3km (1.8 miles) from the gates of Knockdrin you reach a roundabout, where you turn left onto the N4. Kinnegad is less than 20km (12 miles) to the east, and you may arrive there just in time for high tea at the Cottage Restaurant.

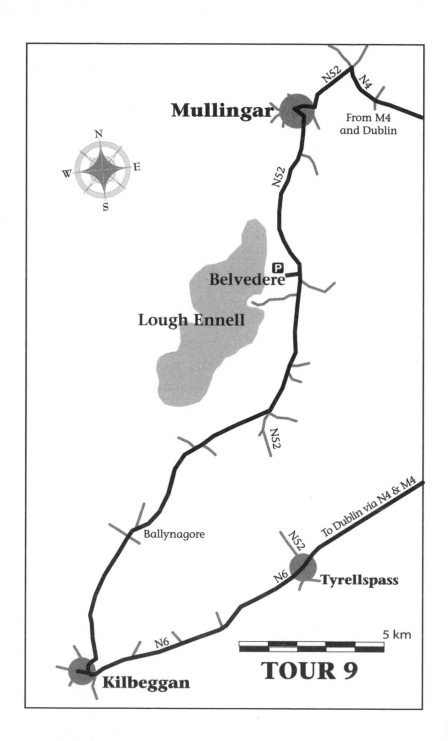

TOUR 9

Mullingar, Belvedere House, Gardens and Park, and the Kilbeggan Museum of Whiskey

A bustling midlands town, a fine Georgian country house and an eighteenth-century whiskey manufactory are the diverse elements of this tour, touching on aspects of canal communications, women's place in eighteenth-century society and the ingenuity of water-powered industrial technology. This is quite a long trip, and Mullingar, Belvedere and Kilbeggan can easily fill your day, so I do not list any 'along the way' distractions.

ROUTE: **The N4 and M4 (toll: E2.50) to Mullingar, the N52 south to Kilbeggan, with the return via the N6, M4 and N4.**

DISTANCE: **210km (130 miles).**

MAPS: **OS Discovery numbers 50, 49, 41 and 48.**

Exit the M50 at intersection 7 (Lucan) and drive west for Mullingar, following the N4 and the M4 all the way. After about 77km (48 miles), on the Mullingar bypass, watch out for a sign for the town centre and take the exit that brings you into town by way of the N52. The centre of Mullingar town is a mile-long main street; there is a number of small car parks nearby (40c per hour).

Although the great chariot road between Uisnach (a royal residence site in the second century) and Tara passed through here, the town of Mullingar, sited on the River Brosna, didn't begin to develop until the thirteenth century when it became a Pale outpost for the Anglo-Normans, who had settled County Meath. The Augustinians established a priory here in 1227 and ten years later the Dominicans established a friary. The town became an important commercial hub in the early nineteenth century upon the completion of the Royal Canal, which was the means of distributing goods from the Shannon and Dublin into the surrounding countryside, and drew produce from the same catchment area for transport to Limerick, via the Shannon, and to Dublin. As a result the town, which until then had been a quiet rural centre, began to enjoy a new prosperity, which has continued up to modern times.

Today, although the commercial use of the Royal Canal has long ago ceased, Mullingar is a bustling country town at the centre of a highly productive agricultural hinterland, and for such a small place is served by a surprisingly wide variety of good quality shops. It is the birthplace of the traditional music festival known as the Fleadh Ceoil, the inaugural event being held here in 1951. Echoes of this tradition can be heard in places like the Temple Bar in Mount Street, where there are live music sessions on Sunday mornings, so if you are unfortunate enough to get here on a wet Sunday, well … every cloud has a silver lining!

James Joyce set parts of *Stephen Hero* in Mullingar, no doubt inspired by a short visit he made to the town in 1901 when his father was compiling the local electoral register. This brief visit is marked by a statue of Joyce in the Greville Arms hotel on Oliver Plunkett Street, a cosy place that is good for coffee, refreshments, or a substantial lunch.

There used to be two good local museums in the town that were open to the public: the Military Museum and the Ecclesiastical Museum. Only the latter can be visited now, and then only on request, but it does have on display a fine collection of hand-carved Penal crosses and the vestments worn by St Oliver Plunkett. If you wish to arrange a visit, make your enquiries at the Tourist Office, which is housed in a carefully converted eighteenth-century market house on Oliver Plunkett Street. Mullingar is a pleasant place to stroll around, and well worth noting are the many fine Georgian doorcases and traditional shopfronts, including the rare Art Nouveau example at Swarbrigg's Shop and a well-restored traditional shopfront at No. 23 Oliver Plunkett Street.

All Saints Church in Church Lane probably dates to the seventeenth century, but utilises some stonework from an original thirteenth-century

Augustinian monastery. In its bell-tower is one of the largest church bells in Ireland, cast by Murphys of Dublin: it weighs nearly an eighth of a ton. The Cathedral of Christ the King at the top of Mary Street dates from 1939 and was designed by Ralph Byrne on the Basilican model. It has sculptural work by Albert Power (the tympanum over the entrance) and H. Thompson (the head of Moses over the main door), and the unusual mosaic work in the Chapel of St Patrick is by the Russian artist Boris Arrep.

———

Leaving Mullingar, follow the N52 southwards, following signs for Belvedere. There is little warning that you have reached it, so keep an eye out for the gates of the estate on the right about 6.4km (4 miles) outside the town.

Belvedere House, Park and Gardens is owned and operated by Westmeath County Council and is a credit to them. (Opening hours: May–August, Monday–Friday, 9.30am–6.00pm; Saturday–Sunday, 10.30am–7.00pm; September–October daily, 10.30am–6.00pm; November–April, 10.30am–4.30pm. Website: *www.belvedere-house.ie*.) For value for money, I have found few similar attractions can equal it. The whole package, including a tour of the house, the run of the grounds, including woodland and lakeside walks, excellent playgrounds, an audio-visual display, exhibitions and a fine café and shop, costs €6 per person. The entire place is wheelchair- and buggy/pram-friendly. A long, pleasantly landscaped avenue leads you to a car park, which in turn leads by path to the visitor's centre, located at the base of the famous 'Jealous Wall'.

Belvedere House was built around 1740 and has been attributed to Richard Castle, one of the most prolific and influential architects of the period. Among his other many commissions in Ireland that still survive are Leinster House in Dublin, Westport House in Westport and Carton House in County Kildare. The name Belvedere is derived from the Italian words *bello*, or beautiful, and *vedere*, or look, together meaning 'beautiful view', which refers to the grand vista the house enjoys of Lough Ennell, its islands and far shore, all framed by fine trees. The original owner was Robert Rochfort, who lived at Gaulstown, 3.6km (2 miles) away, and he built the house as a fishing lodge 'retreat'.

Robert Rochfort's first wife died within a year of their marriage, and the story of his second marriage, to sixteen-year-old Mary Molesworth, provides a glimpse of the status of women, and particularly of wives, in the society of the time. She gave him a daughter and three sons in a short few years, but Rochfort neglected his wife and family, spending most of his time in Dublin, or at the court of King George II in London. After eight years of marriage Rochfort accused his wife of adultery with his brother, Arthur, in what became one of the great scandals of the eighteenth century. Although Mary initially denied the charge, she eventually pleaded guilty in court. Such was the power of a husband over his wife at the time—she was but a possession—Rochfort had Mary imprisoned in his home at Gaulstown. He then moved to Belvedere, where he enjoyed a bachelor existence. She was deprived of all social contact and although her children were allowed to visit her occasionally and she could walk in the grounds, she was not allowed to leave the estate. She did escape once, however, and made her way to Dublin to plead with her father to help her, but he refused and returned her to her husband, who locked her into the house at Gaulstown, removed her personal servants and prevented any further contact with her children. She endured this life for thirty years in all until, on the death of Rochfort, she was rescued by her eldest son, the new Lord Belvedere.

The Belvedere visitors' centre is based in the converted stables of the house. Here you can see an interactive display on the flora and fauna of the estate and Lough Ennell and, in a small cinema, watch a dramatised video of the story of Mary Molesworth. The courtyard has been roofed over in glass to create a pleasant restaurant and permanent exhibition area; off the courtyard is a series of facilities, including a craft shop and a gallery that traces the life and times of the various owners of Belvedere. A well-equipped playground is provided outside, and children will enjoy the donkeys and Shetland ponies in the adjacent animal sanctuary.

Towering over the visitors' centre is the 'Jealous Wall', one of the most impressive folly buildings in Ireland. Measuring 60m long and over 18m high, there are many stories about the reasons for its construction.

Although it could have been put there purely as a folly, as was the fashion of the time, given the character of Robert Rochfort it is also possible that it was placed there to block the view of nearby Tudenham, a house also designed by Richard Castle and built by Rochfort's other brother, George, with whom he had quarrelled. From the south side of the wall you can see the chimneys of the now ruined Tudenham, peeping over the tops of the trees.

The Jealous Wall, Belvedere

One of the last occupants of Belvedere was Charles Howard-Bury, who in 1912 inherited both the Belvedere estate and Charleville Forest Castle outside Tullamore. He was a renowned explorer and in the early twentieth century was one of the few westerners familiar with south-eastern Russia, South China, India and Tibet. He fought in World War One, seeing active service at the Battles of the Somme, Passchendale and Ypres, was captured, escaped, was captured again and ended the war in captivity. In 1920 he was chosen by the Royal Geographic Society to lead the first reconnaissance and detailed survey of Mount Everest and its surrounding mountains. One of the young explorers on his team was George Leigh-Mallory, who was to die in an attempt to conquer the mountain three years later. Howard-Bury took a particular interest in Irish affairs and was involved in the negotiations to have the Hugh Lane art collection sent back to Dublin, where it can still be seen in the Dublin City Gallery The Hugh Lane on Parnell Square.

Now in the ownership of Westmeath County Council, Belvedere has been beautifully restored to its former glory, although the contents were sold in the 1960s. Included in the €6 tariff is a guided tour of the house—a treat not to be missed, particularly if you are lucky enough to get Bridget Geoghegan as a guide as there is little she doesn't know about the place. Of particular interest are the exceptional rococo plasterwork ceilings, featuring flamboyant, swirling clouds and cherubs, the designs of which were created *in situ* rather than made up in panels and fixed in position. The original oak floors look almost new and the inside details of the venetian windows are remarkably fine, and a suitable frame for the wonderful views out over Lough Ennell.

Across rolling lawns scattered with a variety of specimen trees you'll stumble on the wonderfully informal walled garden, sloping easily down from one corner to another and filled with a mixture of new plants and some of the original roses amidst thickly planted herbaceous borders. A lily pond, a wishing well and the perfumes of the blossoms add to the magic of the place. A bright red 'tram' is available to provide regular guided tours of the gardens, and again the price is included in your €6 entrance fee. There are picnic tables along the lakeshore for those who 'bring their own', and a choice of three walks through the estate.

The Molesworth Trail takes about fifteen minutes and circles the house and nearby lawns. The Stream of Life Trail takes about thirty minutes and takes in the lakeshore and the Belvedere stream. The Earl's Trail takes up to an hour and circles the demesne. It sets off along the lakeshore then loops back, passing the Gothic Arch, another eighteenth-century folly, and the Ice House, where 200 years ago ice was made and stored in wintertime for the production of sorbets and ice creams for the dinner table.

Leaving Belvedere, turn right onto the main road and drive south on the N52 for Kilbeggan, under 24km (15 miles) away. Nearly 5km (3 miles) from the gates of Belvedere bear right at a junction, continuing towards Kilbeggan. You will pass the pretty hamlet of Ballynagore, picturesquely sited on the River Brosna, and soon after Kilbeggan Racecourse, before reaching the town of Kilbeggan.

Locke's Distillery is on the main street, just beyond the bridge over the River Brosna. Opening hours: April–October daily, 9.00am–6.00pm; November–March, 10.00am–4.00pm. Website: *www.lockesdistillerymuseum.com.*

Here at Locke's Whiskey Distillery the River Brosna was harnessed in 1757 to provide the power for one of the earliest licensed pot-still distilleries in the world. Although the €5 entrance fee seems a lot after the very good value of Belvedere, it is worth it just to see and appreciate what the combination of man's ingenuity and nature can achieve. A massive, but somewhat dilapidated waterwheel, slowly turned by the waters of the Brosna, runs a bewildering series of cogwheels, shafts and belt drives which are spread through the warren of timber floors of the mill building, the whole creaking and rattling and groaning like a live thing: altogether an experience not to be missed.

At the end of your tour of the works you are treated to a tiny sip of Kilbeggan whiskey, and the opportunity to buy more. There is a pleasant little pub on the premises and a restaurant. The strange-looking, concertina-shaped warehouse one can see from the road is a unique example of a structure using the Ctesiphon (pronounced 'tessifon') technique, called after the Great Arch of Ctesiphon in Baghdad, which, although built of brick, has lasted over 1,600 years, including surviving recent modern warfare. The building here is constructed from unreinforced concrete and the folded, or corrugated, form provides the strength. The technique was invented by Jim Waller (1884–1968)—a Tasmanian of Irish family who studied engineering in Ireland—as a cheap form of building that could be used to rebuild war-damaged Europe and to build the emerging countries of Africa.

Return to Dublin via the N6, the N4 and M4; for *en route* meals or refreshments I recommend the restored fifteenth-century Tyrellspass Castle, which is on the left before you enter the pretty village of Tyrellspass, nearly 10km (6 miles) from Kilbeggan. Alternatively, I would recommend the cosy and comfortable Cottage Café, on the corner of the main street in Kinnegad, where you re-connect with the N4 to return to Dublin.

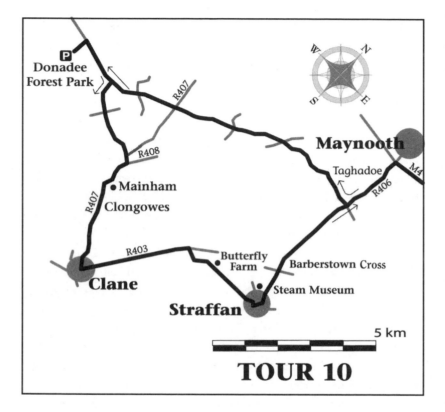

Donadee
Forest Park

R407

R408

R407

Mainham
Clongowes

R403

Clane

Butterfly
Farm

Straffan

Steam Museum

Barberstown Cross

Taghadoe

R406

Maynooth

M4

5 km

TOUR 10

Donadee Forest Park, and the Butterfly Farm and Steam Museum at Straffan

◝◟

D onadee Forest Park is an old, mixed woodland demesne with nature trails, while the spectacular crop of live exotic butterflies at the Butterfly Farm has to be seen to be believed. Our final stop of the day, Straffan steam museum, has a unique collection of engines, some of which can be seen in motion.

ROUTE: **The M4 is followed into Kildare, where a series of side roads takes you to Donadee. The return is made via Mainham churchyard and Clane to Straffan, and then back along the M4 to Dublin.**

DISTANCE: **66km (41 miles).**

MAPS: **OS Discovery numbers 50 and mainly 49.**

Leaving the M50 at intersection 7 (Lucan), a dual carriageway takes you to the M4 motorway, which crosses the River Liffey nearly 8km (5 miles) out. Leave the M4 at intersection 3, signed for Maynooth, and at the roundabout take the R406, signed for Naas. About 2km (1.2 miles) along this road, just before a large ESB station, turn right and after a short distance you will pass the ruined Taghadoe Church and Round Tower on the right. The tower is built on the site of a monastery founded by St Tua, and the church has four castellated corner piers, a Gothic door and windows; the use of brick linings suggests an eighteenth-century date.

The road winds onward, bordered by the well-trimmed hedges that are characteristic of County Kildare. Go straight through the various crossroads you meet, but at 25km (16 miles) from the M50 you will join a slightly 'mainer' road. Carry on straight, and soon the gates to Donadee Forest Park appear on the left: there is an extensive car park at the end of the driveway.

Admission to the Forest Park is €5 per car between May and October; out of season I found there was no charge.

Donadee Forest Park was once the private demesne of the Aylmer family and it really has something for everyone. There is a Nature Trail that winds through the various man-made and natural elements of the woods, and a much shorter Shrubbery Trail that takes you through the shrubs and trees that were planted in the nineteenth century, mainly the evergreen holm oak, horse chestnut, that great Californian redwood the Sequoia, and copper beech, which are seen at their best in early summer. One great stand of beech trees, planted in the early nineteenth century, covers an area of about a hectare. The intricate network of paths and the lack of long views make this place a Mecca for orienteering fanatics, particularly school groups. Some of the paths are suitable for wheelchairs and are marked as such.

In early summer and in autumn the park is remarkable for the intensity of the birdsong that can be heard; all day long a symphony of sweet trills and calls rings through the trees and around the ruined castle.

There is a large pond that has mallards all year round, and occasional visits from mute swans. Coots (with white markings on their beaks) and moorhens (with red beaks) can also be seen and their raucous, unmusical calls echo in the reeds that margin the pond.

In the trees look out for red and grey squirrels, which I am told still co-exist here, and the flashy blue jay. The jay is a shy bird and very similar to its cousin, the magpie, but much more colourful. His call sounds like the magpie squawk, but is gentler. In areas of open, particularly boggy ground, if you are very lucky, you might spot one of Ireland's rarely seen birds, the woodcock. Once disturbed, it will take off suddenly with a great clattering of wings.

There is a considerable number of interesting buildings in the park, many in a ruinous condition. The little neo-Gothic church is perhaps the best-preserved structure and it is still used for Sunday services. Attached to the church is the mausoleum of the Aylmer family. Should you be lucky enough to find it open, inside there is an interesting canopied tomb depicting the kneeling figures of Sir Gerald Aylmer and his wife, Dame Julia Nugent, built nearly 500 years ago in 1626. It also has carved images of the Crucifixion, the Blessed Virgin and various saints. The tomb was moved into the present church from the original church on the site, the sparse ivy-covered ruins of which can be found nearby in the graveyard.

Dominating the centre of the park and now in a state of ruin is Donadee Castle, the former home of the Aylmer family, which they occupied from the fifteenth century until the last of the family, Miss Carolina Aylmer, died in 1935. It boasts a rare assembly of styles and consists of the tower house that was the Aylmers' original home in Kildare and a fortified mansion of 1624, which was reconstructed in 1775. In the early nineteenth century considerable Gothic renovations and additions were carried out, including the tower on the left and the bow-fronted entrance court in the centre, to the designs of one of Ireland's best-known architects of the time, Richard Morrison. The coat of arms of Sir Gerald Aylmer, dated 1624, is mounted on the front wall of the house and a plaque beneath it states the building was destroyed by fire in the war of 1640. The place was 'in the wars' again in 1691, when it was besieged by followers of James II, but the attack was gallantly repulsed by a small garrison led by Lady Ellen, the wife of Sir Thomas Aylmer.

Behind an elaborate wall with a fine wall-walk of cantilevered limestone slabs to the north-east of the old house there are extensive arcaded, early nineteenth-century 'out-offices' and the remnants of a walled garden; almost every building seems to have a stone plaque with a date inscribed, indicating the pride with which the Aylmers developed their property.

There are plenty of places to have a picnic at Donadee, but in summertime there is a tea house that provides snacks.

To continue the tour to Clane, turn right on leaving the gates of Donadee and follow the road east and south to reach the R407 and bear right: after a short distance turn right again at a T-junction. A little more than 1km (0.5 mile) from this junction, on the left at Mainham, there is an interesting old churchyard that is worth visiting. There is space to park at the gate.

Pass through the modern cemetery to reach the old one. Note the difference in ground levels: that in the old cemetery is considerably higher due to hundreds of years of interments there. The ruins of the fifteenth-century Anglo-Norman church, lying under a fine stand of lime trees, are substantial and include the fortifications that were common in places like this, on the borders of The Pale, when attacks by the 'native' Irish were to be expected and feared.

The mausoleum of the Wogan Browne family, built in 1743, lies beside the church. They lived in nearby Castle Browne, a border castle of The Pale until it was sold to the Jesuits in 1813 by General Wogan Browne. He had an interesting European military career, at one time serving as *aide-de-camp* to the King of Saxony. Soldiering abroad was a family trait: an earlier member, Charles Wogan, was a soldier of fortune who fought in the Stuart rising in 1715, and afterwards served in France and Spain. His success led to his conferral as a Roman Senator by the Pope, and eventually he was made Governor of the province of La Mancha.

In the adjoining field is a much overgrown motte, or earthen castle, this one built by the first Anglo-Norman lord in this area, John de Hereford. It is known locally as Queen Buan's Grave and is marked as such on earlier Ordnance maps. In the legends, Queen Buan was the beautiful wife of the King of Leinster, Meas Geaghra. He was killed and decapitated by the Ulster warrior Conal Cearnach in a battle on the banks of the nearby Liffey. Conal then abducted Queen Buan, but when he boastfully displayed her late husband's head, she got such a fright that she died. It is said she was buried here, with her husband's head. There is also evidence that this place was important in pre-Norman times when it was used as an *Aenach,* or assembly site, for the Kings of Leinster, a place where all the local chiefs and their followers would gather periodically for games and feasting—an ancient form of social networking. In many cases, early Norman colonisers occupied existing important sites and often saved labour by making use of existing features or mounds to build their mottes. It is possible, therefore, that Queen Buan and her unfortunate husband's head may indeed lie beneath this grassy mound.

Leaving Mainham, a little further on, on the left, you will meet the imposing Gothic gates of Clongowes Wood College, the well-known Jesuit boarding school. At the end of the long, tree-lined driveway the original house with its battlemented towers can be seen, now forming the nucleus of the college. This was Castle Browne until 1813, and dates from the early eighteenth century, but it was substantially altered in 1788 in the Gothic Revival style.

A short distance further on you enter the village of Clane.

Turn left at the crossroads in the town, following the sign for Straffan. Nearly 4.8km (3 miles) from Clane, turn right at a crossroads. After a couple of sharp bends the road goes straight towards Straffan. Look out on the left for the Straffan Butterfly Farm; there is ample car parking on-site.

Straffan Butterfly Farm: tel: 01 6721109; email: *info@straffanbutter flyfarm.com*; website: *www.straffanbutterflyfarm.com*. Entry fees: family ticket (two adults and three children) €20; adults €7; children €4; senior citizens €4. Open 12 noon–5.30pm during the 'butterfly season', usually from the end of June to August, inclusive.

Butterfly at Straffan

At this wonderful farm you can not only see but walk among live, brilliantly coloured butterflies, both native and foreign, all housed in a special tunnel with a constant tropical climate. It makes for a good stop on a rainy day: in the greenhouse environment you can watch these amazing 'flying flowers' fly and graze all around you in comfortable heat while the rain teems down outside. There are also bird-eating spiders, stick insects, millipedes, giant snails, small reptiles and all kinds of creepy-crawlies that children cringe at, but love to see. There is a picnic area and all the displays are wheelchair accessible.

Leaving the butterflies behind, continue towards Straffan, on the right passing the impressive gates to the K Club, an exclusive golf and country club.

After a short distance you'll come upon the village of Straffan, at a T-junction. On the left, in an overgrown graveyard, is the ruined pre-Penal church of Straffan, the tower of which, with its double belfry, provided the living quarters for the priest—the late medieval version of 'living over the shop'. Opposite is the 'modern' church of Straffan, its very slender, pinnacled spire more reminiscent of Prague than Kildare.

Turn left at this T-junction and shortly after turn right at the pub and a couple of hundred metres along, on the right, you'll find the Steam Museum and Gardens in the grounds of Lodge Park.

Straffan Steam Museum and Walled Gardens: tel: 01 6273155 or 01 6288412; e-mail: *info@steam-museum.ie*; website: *www.steam-museum.ie*. Admission: adults €7.50; children/OAPs/students/groups of twenty or more, €5; family admission €20. Open: June–September.

Lodge Park is a fine Palladian house built in 1777, consisting of a central block with four wings, or pavilions, instead of the two that was usual in that period. It is owned by the Guinness family, and the nearby Steam Museum was established some years ago by the late Richard Guinness. The building that houses the museum is a kind of museum piece itself: it used to be a church sited in Inchicore in Dublin, but after lying disused for some time it was dismantled and re-erected, stone by stone, here in Straffan.

There is a fascinating array of steam engines on display, from trains—including Ireland's first commuter train, which ran on Ireland's first railway line from Westland Row to Dún Laoghaire—to all kinds of industrial engines. In addition, there are models of trains and fully operative steam engine models that are fascinating to watch.

The walled garden was first planted in 1777, and was restored recently. In it you will find vegetables and fruits grown for the house, herbaceous borders, box hedges and a circular *rosarie*. A tea house serves tea and home-made cakes.

Leaving the Steam Museum, turn left onto the public road and return to the village. Turn right in the village and head north, passing straight through Barberstown Cross, reaching the M4 again for the journey back to Dublin.

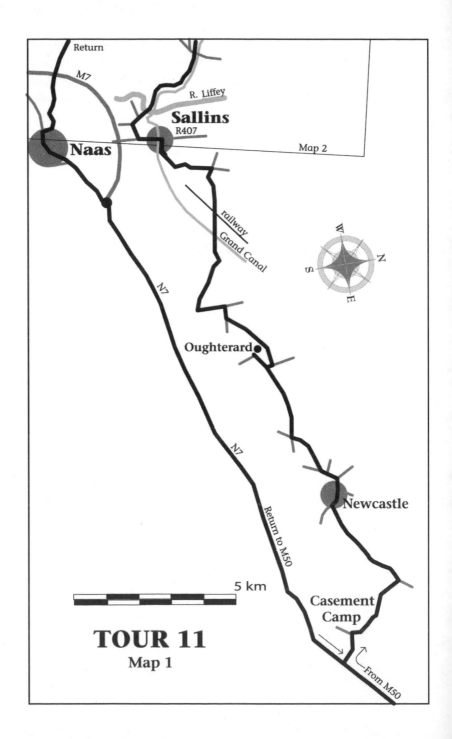

Return

M7

R. Liffey

Sallins
R407

Map 2

Naas

railway

Grand Canal

N7

Oughterard

N7

Return to M50

Newcastle

5 km

Casement
Camp

From M50

TOUR 11
Map 1

TOUR 11

Kildare's Canals and Bogs

⚜

This tour takes you into the heart of County Kildare to the burial place of Arthur Guinness, and along canal banks to reach the eastern edge of the great Bog of Allen, an appropriate site for the National Peatland Centre. Nearby is Lullymore Heritage Park, after a visit to which the tour returns to Dublin via Robertstown and Naas.

ROUTE: **After a brief run on the N7, the route leads by side roads to Newcastle, Oughterard and Sallins to reach Lullymore. The return is made by Robertstown and Naas and via the N7 to Dublin.**

DISTANCE: **120km (72 miles).**

MAPS: **OS Discovery numbers 49 and 50.**

Leave the M50 at intersection 9 (the Red Cow) and head south on the N7: after about 5km (3 miles) turn off, following the signs for Blessington, Baldonnel and City West Campus. Crossing a dual carriageway, follow the signs for Baldonnel. The road follows the east and then the north perimeter of Casement Camp, HQ of the Irish Air Corps, still shown on the maps with its 1930s name: Baldonnel Aerodrome. The airfield has been in use since it was established as the Headquarters of the Irish Wing of the Royal Air Force late in the First World War. It was handed over to the Free State in 1922, and with just one aircraft—an old Martynside biplane that had been purchased by Michael Collins—two pilots and a rundown airfield, the Irish Army Air Service was ushered into existence.

Many historic aviation events took place at Baldonnel. In April 1928 the *Bremen*, the first plane to complete an east–west crossing of the Atlantic, took off from its runway. It was piloted by Captain Hermann

Koehl, a German pilot, and the co-pilot on the historic flight was Colonel James Fitzmaurice, then Commanding Officer of the Irish Army Air Corps. The first Aer Lingus scheduled flight took off from here in May 1936, when five passengers were carried to Bristol by a two-engined De Havilland biplane called the *Iolar*.

Past the main gates to Casement Camp, look out on the left for the staff and family quarters, which present good and rare surviving examples of 1930s Irish architecture. At the T-junction about 1km (0.5 mile) past the gates, go left for Newcastle. After just over 3km (2 miles), turn right to enter the old village, which dates back to the time of the Norman conquest.

Of interest here is the Old Rectory, situated on the right beyond the church, a neat, five-bay, early eighteenth-century house. There is an old yew tree in the garden under which the author of *Gulliver's Travels*, Dean Jonathan Swift, is said to have sat while visiting the then owners. Next to the Old Rectory is the ruin of the original church of Newcastle, beyond which is St Finian's Church of Ireland church, a medieval building with a large residential tower attached.

At the end of the village, by McAvoy's pub (in ruins after a fire at time of writing), follow the main road left. Take the second turn right after a short distance and follow the road as it climbs the western side of Athgoe Hill. As it levels out, the grassy sward of Lyons Hill, with a line of trees running over its northern side, comes into view to the right. This is a very historic place. Note the plateau-shape of what is possibly

The Bremen *taking off from Baldonnel*

an Iron Age enclosure on the top; this is said to be an ancient place of assembly of the Leinster kings. It is said that St Conleth, a hermit and metalworker who was appointed by St Brigid as chaplain to her nuns in Kildare, was attacked and killed by a pack of wolves on this hillside. Later the Ui Dunchada clan had their headquarters here, until they were driven out by the Norsemen of Dublin.

Go right at the crossroads and cross into County Kildare, then descend into a townland named Pluckstown; the next townland to the south is called Banshee. There are great views to the left across north Kildare and south Dublin, and to the right stretches the long demesne wall of Lyons House, a great mansion built by the Cloncurry family in 1797, which served as their home for most of the following 150 years. The pillars of the portico have an interesting history. Three of them originated in the Golden House, built in Rome by Emperor Nero in the middle of the first century AD. They were removed from there by the artist and architect Raphael in the early sixteenth century to decorate the glorious Renaissance Palazzo Farnese. The scientist and explorer Baron von Humboldt bought them in the early nineteenth century as a present for the King of Prussia, but later changed his mind and sold them to Lord Cloncurry, who brought them back from Rome and re-erected them in the portico. The founder of Ryanair, Tony Ryan, is the current owner of the house and demesne.

Ahead the truncated round tower of Oughterard comes into view: carry on straight past a turn to the right and watch out for the entrance to the churchyard on the right-hand side. There is space to park on the road. A pleasant gravel driveway leads to the ruined church and graveyard. The first vault you come across is the family tomb of the Wolfe family of nearby Furness House. The wider Wolfe family produced many historic figures: General James Wolfe, the eighteenth-century soldier who was killed at the Battle of Quebec in 1759, and the Rev. Charles Wolfe, who wrote the well-known elegy 'The Burial of Sir John Moore'. Distinguished lawyer and politician Theobald Wolfe of Blackhall was godfather to the revolutionary Theobald Wolfe Tone, whose father was the Blackhall coachbuilder.

The round tower, with its doorway 4m from the ground, marks the site of a sixth-century monastery. The church is roofed with barrel-vaulted stone and dates from the sixteenth century. A stair tower leans, Pisa-like, away from the main building, propped up by a couple of modern struts. Taking due care you can climb the rickety stairs from inside the church (children love it!) and get out onto the roof, a vantage point that affords great views all around, from the plains of Kildare to the south and west, around to the foothills of the Dublin and Wicklow Mountains, across to the nearby Knockaniller to the east and Lyons Hill to the north-east. Near the church you will find the plaque commemorating 'universally loved and respected' Arthur Guinness, (1725–1803), who is buried in a nearby vault. West of the church there is a spooky underground vault, partially open to the sky.

In March 1815 'The Liberator', Daniel O'Connell, made a speech in which he called Dublin Corporation 'beggarly', which pronouncement led to him being challenged to a duel by John d'Esterre, a member of the Corporation. The dual, with pistols, was fought somewhere in the fields outside the churchyard here, and during it d'Esterre was mortally wounded.

Returning to the car, go back the way you came and take the first turn to the left and almost immediately go left again. Just over 2km (1.2 miles) on, go right at a T-junction and turn left shortly after. In less than 1km (0.5 mile), turn right again: soon you cross the Grand Canal and shortly thereafter the railway. At the next cross, Sherlockstown Crossroads, turn left for Sallins.

Sallins is a pleasant village with the Grand Canal harbour at its centre, usually lined with colourful barges and cruisers and overlooked by the Bridgewater Inn and the Shanghai Restaurant. The village owes its existence to the canal, which reached this far from Dublin in 1780.

Pass the Shanghai Restaurant, swing right and immediately left onto the main road, the R407, to cross over the canal. About 700m on, after the speed limit sign, take a right turn. Reaching the Naas branch of the Grand Canal, turn right again, and after a sharp bend to the left, turn off immediately, with care, to the right onto a narrow road. Pass under a railway bridge to reach and follow the towpath of the Grand Canal.

You are now following in the footsteps, or should I say the hoofprints, of the many thousands of horses that drew canal barges along here between 1780 and the early twentieth century, transporting passengers, coal, building materials, stout and other goods from Dublin into the midlands and agricultural produce, bricks and more passengers from the midlands back into Dublin.

Follow the towpath as it and the canal pass over the River Liffey by way of the Leinster Aqueduct, a five-arch stone marvel of eighteenth-century engineering. The Liffey, which rises just 24km (15 miles) from Dublin, flows a long, looping 147km (92 miles) through Wicklow and Kildare before it actually passes through the city and flows out into Dublin Bay.

The towpath continues along a pleasant, tree-lined stretch that is popular for walking and angling. Just past a picturesque cottage on the left, look out for Sandymount House on the far side of the canal. This fine Georgian country house was recently owned by a member of The Rolling Stones rock group, and locals say he had a complete pub installed in the house as part of the renovations. At Digby Bridge, named, as most of the early canal bridges were, after one of the original shareholders, go left and immediately right, and then right again to rejoin the canal bank after a few hundred metres.

After a short distance you will approach the seventeenth lock on the Grand Canal at Landenstown Bridge. On the left are the gates to Landenstown Demesne, and two doll's house gatelodges with limestone-pillared porticos and diamond-paned windows. Cross the bridge to the north side of the canal and continue along a fine straight reach of the canal, lined on the south side by the trees of Landenstown Wood. After a little more than 1km (0.6 mile) the road finally leaves the canal behind. A little further along the towpath, here is the eighteenth lock of the Grand Canal, the eighteenth step up from the Liffey and the summit level of the canal. The next lock, 8km (5 miles) further on, is the first of another eighteen locks that take the level of the canal down to the level of the River Shannon, 120km (75 miles) away.

A straight road now takes you into the village of Prosperous, founded and named by Robert Brooke in 1776 to be the centre of a new cotton manufacturing industry, which was anything but prosperous: it failed and was abandoned a few years later. Some of the houses in the village date from that time—the presbytery was once the residence of Matthew Tone, a coffin-maker and brother of Theobald Wolfe Tone.

When you reach the main street, turn left and continue on out the long straight road towards the peat bogs of Kildare and Offaly. This length of road—part of one of the first planned highways in Ireland and built in 1751—is one of the longest stretches of straight road in the country: but for a shortage of funds it would have carried on a full 23km (14 miles) to Ballinagar in County Offaly. After 7km (4.4 miles) the village of Allenwood is reached: 1km (0.6 mile) beyond the village bear left over Shee Bridge, which crosses the Grand Canal obliquely, and continue on, following signs for Lullymore Heritage Park.

Soon the road enters into an extensive area of raised peat bog on the edge of the great Bog of Allen. All around are peat workings where the material is harvested for the manufacture of peat briquettes for fuel. A short distance into the bog you'll come upon an area called Lullymore, formerly an island whose surface was a few feet above the surrounding bog, and here you will find the Bog of Allen Nature Centre and the National Peatland Centre. They are housed in an old stable block formerly belonging to Lullymore House. (The National Peatland Centre: tel: 045 860133; website: *www.ipcc.ie*)

The Irish Peatland Conservation Council is a national charity and is largely supported by private donations from supporters. In October 2003 it purchased this two-acre site and set about turning the buildings and land into a major peatland interpretive centre. It is a showcase for the bogs, fens, wetlands and cutaway bogs characteristic of the renowned Bog of Allen and other Irish bogs. By staging exhibitions and carrying out experiments the Council hopes to lead visitors on an exciting adventure in conservation and help them to understand the environmental importance of wetland sites and the cultural importance of wetlands to local communities.

Here, you can find out everything you ever wanted to know about Ireland's unique boglands, and can experience samples of our three main wetland habitats—open water, fen marsh and raised bog—all of which have been recreated at the centre and are typical of the past, present and future landscape of the Bog of Allen.

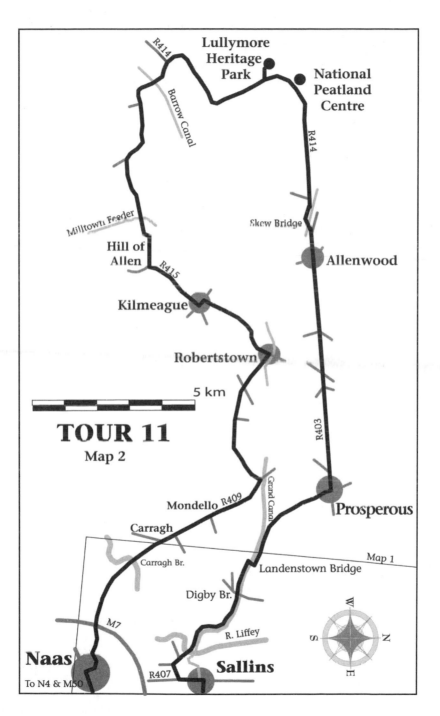

R414

Lullymore
Heritage
Park

National
Peatland
Centre

Barrow Canal

R414

Milltown Feeder

Skew Bridge

Hill of
Allen

R415

Allenwood

Kilmeague

Robertstown

5 km

TOUR 11

Map 2

R403

Mondello R409

Grand Canal

Prosperous

Carragh

Carragh Br.

Map 1

Landenstown Bridge

Digby Br.

R. Liffey

M7

Naas

To N4 & M50

R407

Sallins

The indoor visitor centre has permanent exhibitions that highlight human interaction with boglands in Ireland, the conservation of habitats, flora and fauna, and the cultural aspects of boglands. Just in case this sounds too serious, there are also opportunities for young children to get their hands dirty in a pond zone where they can interact with 'all things wet and wild'. Another exhibit that is sure to interest children is the Fly Traps Hothouse, where you can see a collection of carnivorous plants from other parts of the world.

For those interested in gardening, and particularly gardening in a sustainable way, there is a composting and recycling garden, showing new ways of doing things with ideas that everyone can use at home, a birds and wildlife garden, and a bog garden.

A Peatlands Research Centre has also been set up here and is equipped with a research library, providing reference resources for studying the conservation, interpretation, folklore, archaeology, utilisation and management of peatlands around the world. A comprehensive database contains information on peatlands, a resource that is valuable for both conservation and education.

The centre is wheelchair accessible, and additional attractions include an art gallery, a restaurant, a shop and garden plant centre. There are also nice picnic areas.

Regular events and courses are organised, but as it is, in the main, a result of voluntary effort, some of the events, such as maintenance work on the Carnivorous Plant Display, potting of plants and bulbs, hedge planting, tree planting and setting up bird-boxes, depend on the public getting involved and donating their time and labour. In return, there is a lot to be learned about these subjects from the Centre's experts. Booking for these events and courses is essential: it would be wise to check by telephone in advance. The Centre is open from Monday to Friday all year around; Saturdays and Sundays are reserved for large, pre-booked groups.

Leave the Peatland Centre and drive the short distance to the main road again. On the corner, where you turn in to the Centre, is a monument to Captain John Doorley. At an early age he got involved in the United Irishmen, and quickly rose through the ranks to become the leader of the rebels in this area during the 1798 Rebellion. He led the attack on Rathangan and had a reward of £100 put on his head by the British authorities. Eventually they caught up with him as he tried to swim the Boyne in a bid to escape, and he was taken to Mullingar. Before his clothes had even dried out after his swim, they say, he was hanged. The monument to Doorley incorporates some cross-incised stones that were found in the nearby ancient Lullymore graveyard.

Turn right, and continue along the road for 1km (0.6 mile) before turning right again and following a sign for the Lullymore Heritage Park, which is a short distance down a side road.

Lullymore Heritage Park (website: *www.Kildare.ie/tourism/sites/lullymore;* tel: 045 870238 to confirm opening hours and current entrance fee) is designed for children and has many attractions of interest to all ages. There is a large playground, a crazy golf course and a theme park that includes miniature versions of historic sites, such as Newgrange. There is a Bog Walk that takes you through woodland and bogland, where you will find thatched dwellings of the type used in the Neolithic age, and a cottage made entirely from sods of turf, which gives a good idea of how most of the people of this area lived in the nineteenth century, and indeed well into the twentieth century.

A large mock train provides regular tours around the Park. In an industrial building there is an exhibition area displaying artefacts of local heritage, and it also houses another playground, called a Funky Forest, where children can have a lot of fun, even if the weather is bad.

These and the lots of other attractions available should keep children and adults happily occupied for up to three or four hours. The entrance fee covers all the facilities: there is also a cafeteria and a craft shop, where, among other souvenirs, you can buy turned wooden bowls and lamps made from 10,000-year-old bog oak.

Leaving Lullymore Heritage Park, turn right onto the main road and head out across the eastern edge of the Bog of Allen, a vast area of land that, apart from the odd track, drain or copse of trees, is almost a blank on the map. After 4km (2.5 miles) bear left off the main road, following a sign for the Grand Canal. You will hardly notice crossing over the Slate River, which, although it rises near Prosperous, does not take its waters the obvious route to the sea by way of the wandering Liffey, but instead flows eventually into the River Barrow at Monasterevin, and then on to Waterford Harbour some 128km (80 miles) away. The Grand Canal is crossed below the twenty-second Lock, and a little over 2.5km (1.5 miles) further on, turn left towards the Hill of Allen: at 219m above sea level, it one of Kildare's few high points.

The hill—partly dismembered to provide the gravel for the concrete to build Celtic Tiger Ireland—is the location of the legendary camp of Finn Mc Cumhaill and the Fianna, Ireland's ancient standing army, who seemed to have had little to do most of the time but range across the country, hunting and carousing. A battle was fought here in AD 722 during which, legend has it, 9,000 Ulster warriors were killed, including a bard who continued singing after he had been beheaded! The tower on the hill was built by the local landlord, Sir Gerald Aylmer, in 1859. It can be viewed with the permission of the quarry owners, Roadstone. What I found particularly interesting were the inscriptions—which you'll find on each of the steps of the internal spiral staircase—of the names of all those who worked to erect the tower, including five women.

The Milltown Feeder canal is crossed next: this canal, fed from the Pollardstown Fen, supplies the Grand Canal with its water, which flows into the system at Robertstown, then divides to flow east to the Irish Sea and west to the Shannon.

At the next crossroads turn left onto the R415 and ascend the hill to pass through the hamlet of Allen, and after 1.5km (1 mile) you'll meet the pleasant village of Kilmeague, with its unusual battlemented church tower. Turn left at the crossroads, and then turn immediately right past the church.

Robertstown, a Grand Canal harbour that owes its origination and continued existence to the canal, is reached 2.5km (1.6 miles) further on. This peaceful village is overlooked by a great old hotel, which was built in 1799 to cater for those travelling east to Dublin, or west to the

Shannon by fly-boat. It is one of the few such buildings to survive more or less intact.

Follow the road around in front of the hotel and then away from the canal, continuing straight for just over 4km (2.4 miles), and turn right onto the R409. Soon the walls of Mondello Motor Racing Track are passed on the right, and the road goes through the village of Carragh. About 0.5km (0.3 mile) outside the village you again cross the River Liffey, this time by Carragh Bridge, which is thought to date from about AD 1500, making it the oldest of the many bridges over the River Liffey.

A further 2.5km (1.5 miles) down the road and you cross the M7, and soon after reach the town of Naas. Take the R445 north out of town to reach the N7 and return to Dublin, re-connecting with the M50 at the Red Cow intersection.

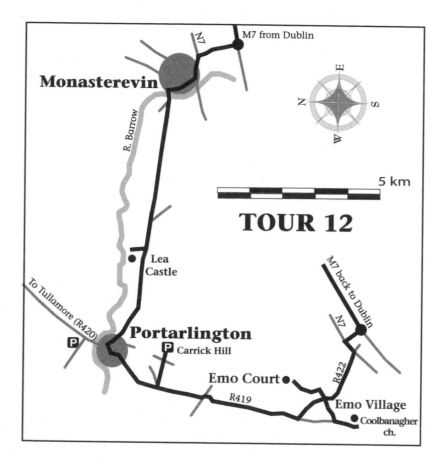

Monasterevin

N7

M7 from Dublin

R. Barrow

5 km

TOUR 12

Lea
Castle

To Tullamore (R420)

P

Portarlington

P Carrick Hill

Emo Court

R419

M7 back to Dublin

N7

R422

Emo Village

Coolbanagher
ch.

TOUR 12

Portarlington and Emo Court

This route brings you into County Laois to visit a town with a French connection and a great house and its gardens. Along the way you can visit the remains of a great castle overlooking the River Barrow and a rural Georgian church, and avail of a short woodland walk or a longer bog walk.

ROUTE: **Exiting the M50 at intersection 9 (the Red Cow), the N7 and M7 are followed south to Monasterevin, from where you take the R424 to Portarlington. The return journey to intersection 9 and Dublin is made via the M7 and N7.**

DISTANCE: **144km (89 miles).**

MAPS: **Mainly OS Discovery number 55.**

Take intersection 9 (Red Cow exit) from the M50 and drive south into County Kildare on the N7 and M7. About 50km (31 miles) from the M50 turn off the M7, following signs for Monasterevin. Less than 3km (1.8 miles) on you'll see the grand castellated gates of Moore Abbey on the left, the house where Count John McCormack lived for a time, heralding your entrance to the town of Monasterevin. Driving down the main street, take the second turn to the right, marked by an elaborate Celtic Revival High Cross that was erected in honour of Fr Prendergast, who was hanged near here for his involvement in the rebellion of 1798. Drive up Drogheda Street, named for the Earls of Drogheda who occupied Moore Abbey and owned the town in the booming years of the early nineteenth century when the canal opened it up for trade. The fine Georgian houses on this street, with their gardens across the road and sweeping down to the banks of the Barrow, were once the homes of the wealthy merchants of the town. In one of these gardens stands a monument to the poet Gerard Manley Hopkins, who used to visit friends in the town. At the end of the street the road passes over the Barrow Canal, which is carried across the River Barrow by a fine aqueduct. Passing under a railway bridge, the road bears left a little further on to cross the river by way of the sixteenth-century Pass Bridge, one of the oldest bridges in Ireland. Note the 'pedestrian refuges'—angular alcoves to allow pedestrians stand out of the way of heavily loaded carts—a feature of such bridges.

Continue on in the direction of Portarlington and pass into County Laois as the road crosses an extensive area where peat bogs have been harvested to feed the power station that used to stand north of Portarlington. For some distance here the road resembles a causeway because it is a couple of metres higher than the surrounding land, which has been stripped of its peat covering. To the left of the road look out for a forlorn bridge that once crossed the now filled-in Mountmellick Canal. Nearly 4km (2.5 miles) from Monasterevin you join the main road and continue on straight. About 800m from the junction, and not far past Portarlington Rugby Football Club grounds, take the turn to the right, off the main road. Almost immediately the tower of Lea Castle appears ahead. The road meanders along, and less than 0.5km (little over 0.25 mile) from the main road you come to a large, disused farmhouse on the left. Just beyond it, on the right, there is space to park, but be careful you don't block the gateway.

To gain access to Lea Castle look for a steel stile about 40m further along the road, on the left. There is a standard notice at the gate to the field stating clearly that the occupier owes no duty of care to anyone entering, but I have met the landowner and he happily showed me how to reach the castle. The ruinous condition of the castle makes it unsuitable for very young children, but older ones, with proper supervision and care, will find it a fascinating place. The field you cross to reach the castle can be wet and boggy in places, so it is worthwhile wearing boots. Follow the hedge, keeping it to your left; over to the right the field is bordered by the swiftly flowing River Barrow. As the river closes in from the right you reach another stile, which takes you into the field where the castle stands.

Lea Castle was probably built about 1260 on the site of an earlier motte, and no doubted intended to control the River Barrow and the surrounding countryside. Subsequently a small town grew up around the castle, but there is now no trace of it. A particularly massive structure, the castle originally had a rectangular keep with a great tower at each corner, each one about 10m diameter, and would have been similar to Carlow Castle, or that at Ferns in County Wexford. The central high 'keep' had a double line of defence: an outer walled courtyard with a double-towered gatehouse, and an inner walled ward. Furthermore, it seems likely that the Barrow was incorporated into some form of defensive moat.

For all its defences, Lea Castle was not a successful place of safety in time of war: it was burned by the local O'Dempsey clan at the end of the thirteenth century, rebuilt, only to be burned again by the marauding Scottish army under Edward Bruce a couple of decades later. It changed hands many times until it was finally 'de-commissioned' nearly 400 years later by contractors paid by Cromwell to 'slight' all castles, that is to make them unusable by destroying the stairs and taking off the roof, often with the aid of explosives.

Once over the second stile, you can gain entry through the outer walls of the castle if you go around to the left and lay siege to the undergrowth. Apart from some of the outer walls and fragments of the gatehouse, only one of the four great towers survives: much of the castle's stones sleep under a series of grass-covered mounds. The first thing that strikes you when you do get inside the walls, however, is the massiveness of the remains: the great stone arches, the enormously thick walls and the great holes blown in the walls by the Cromwellian contractors. It is a massiveness that only hints at the original scale of the castle, and in turn at the power of the armies that conquered it.

It is not easy to decipher the layout of the original complex, but you can find the inner and outer gates and see the slot in the wall where the portcullis might have hung. One windowed, intermural staircase in the great tower survives and you can, with care, clamber up its rough steps to reach a small, grassy platform overhung by a section of arch. It is a good place to sit and take in the surroundings, and perhaps imagine your way back 800 years. Then, the Barrow would have meandered from the west as it does today, but would have been harnessed into a harbour and probably a moat under the walls, and very likely used to turn a watermill. Crohan Hill, the site of the main stronghold of the O'Conor Faly clan from the fourteenth to the eighteenth centuries, peeps over the horizon 50km (31 miles) to the north. The Slieve Bloom Mountains line the horizon to the south-west and the Wicklow range is clear to the east. At the time the castle was built the surrounding landscape would have been thickly wooded, providing the timber for the construction of floors, partitions and roofs, all now disappeared—but one wonders where all the stone came from.

In spite of the destruction, large areas of the stone-vaulted ground floor survive, and in one place there is an example of the technical excellence of medieval wall-builders: a very large section of wall, blown down by Cromwell's explosives, has remained in one piece, the mortar so strong that it has become a massive, inclined floorslab spanning more than 10m.

Back at the car, return to the main road, turn right and Portarlington is reached in less than 2km (just over 1 mile). To the right, off Main Street, and down the grandly titled Park Lane, there is an ample town car park that is free. Opposite the car park is a public park that runs along the banks of the Barrow and which has a very good children's playground. Portarlington is a compact place, and easy to explore on foot.

The town was founded on an important crossing-point of the River Barrow in 1666 by Sir Henry Bennett, Lord Arlington, to house English and other Protestant colonists and to strengthen English influence and control in this midland area, which up until then had been ruled by the O'Dempsey clan. It was a period when the English were encouraging 'planters' from Protestant areas all over Europe to come and settle in Ireland: Rhinelanders came and settled in County Limerick; Quakers in nearby Mountmellick; and Flemish settlers were putting down roots in Wexford, all helping to increase the proportion of the population in Ireland loyal to the Crown. Within a couple of decades Portarlington housed not only English settlers but a thriving colony of Huguenots, refugees from religious persecution in France. They settled well and brought not only an air of sophistication to the place but good schools, one of which was attended by the young Duke of Wellington.

Much of the fabric of the old town of Portarlington has survived thanks to the relative remoteness of the town from the main Dublin–Cork–Limerick routes, which has meant a slower pace of development in the town in the modern period. There are some unfortunate exceptions, but in the main the narrow streets and rich variety of Georgian and Victorian house and shop fronts still bestow a comfortable, traditional character on the town. It is interesting to enumerate the many different styles of doorcase, from chunky mid-eighteenth-century specimens with blocked linings to simple, refined, late Georgian ones with Tuscan columns and delicate fanlights. On Patrick Street and Frenchchurch Street you can find some of the surviving Huguenot houses, which were originally planned in the manner of French towns of the period, with reception rooms facing the gardens and river rather than the street.

There is a town museum in the Catholic Club on Main Street that I am told is very good, but it has very restricted opening hours, only two days a month, so I didn't get to see it! The old French church is worth a visit: the key for the graveyard can be obtained in Fletchers' newsagents at the north end of Main Street, and inside you will find the headstones of some of the early French inhabitants of the town, with names such as Daillon and Desvoeu.

There is a variety of places for lunching, including Matthew's Courtyard Café, off Main Street, where snacks, paninis and sandwiches are the order of the day, the Anvil Inn on Main Street, where more traditional lunches of roast chicken and beef with vegetables are served in enormous portions, and The East End Hotel, an old building, once a school, with some remnants of fine ceilings, where good country cooking is available in the bar.

There are two interesting walks worth trying close to the town: one a short woodland stroll; the other a longer bog and forest walk. For the latter, called the Derryounce Walkway, take the Tullamore Road a few hundred metres north out of town, crossing over the Barrow. Shortly after the bridge go left to reach the start of the walk, which is on the right. An illustrated signboard describes the features of the walk: the full route is 6.5km (4 miles), which should take about eighty minutes, and the pathway takes you out of County Laois and into County Offaly, through forestry, past esker ridges and onto a typical midlands bog before culminating at a peat bog lake, Lough Lurgan. There is also a shorter version of this walk for the time-pressed. Moorhens, curlews and sometimes grouse can be spotted *en route*, and in summertime the ubiquitous skylark fills the air with sweet song.

For the other walk, the woodland stroll, take the Portlaoise road out of the town. A short distance outside the town is the railway track, which you pass over, and then a little over 1km (0.6 mile) after the track, take a turn to the left signed for Monasterevin (near an old 'dry' bridge which crossed the canal that once flowed here), and go immediately right, down a narrow road. Keep on straight through a crossroads and over another railway bridge to reach the car park at wooded Carrick Hill. From the car park it is a short walk (about ten minutes, following white arrows on the trees) by well-trodden pathways to the top of the hill: a particular joy to do in late April or early May when the bluebells are as dense as I have seen anywhere and the newly leafing beeches throw a pale green light over all. At the top of the hill is a strange folly— a round tower with a vaulted, conical roof, built sometime in the eighteenth century to provide assistance during a time of general hardship. Unfortunately, due to the encroachment of the surrounding woods, there is at present no view from the top of the hill.

To get to Emo Court and parkland, take the Portlaoise road out of town. After just under 7km (4.2 miles) you will reach the main Mountmellick road, where you turn left to reach the village of Emo. The turn for Emo Court is on the left, in the middle of the village.

The driveway up to the house is long and for the most part winds through a thick woodland of beeches and birches. When the driveway emerges from the woods and Emo Court appears ahead, it is on the far side of a slight eminence and the approach is such that the house looks quite modest. This is not the formal avenue to the house, however: the 'real' avenue is a much more dramatic affair, being over 1km (0.6 mile) long and corralled by a line of giant sequoias, said to be the longest of its kind. Close to the house there is a car park, with toilets adjacent.

The extensive gardens of Emo Court are open to the public, free of charge, all year round and, like the house, are today in the charge of the State. The formal gardens were originally designed by the eighteenth-century English garden designer Capability Brown, and beyond them the informal gardens stretch off into the far distance and include a twenty-acre, wood-fringed lake.

Built for John Dawson, the First Earl of Portarlington, Emo was begun about 1790 to the designs of James Gandon, the English architect who gave us, among other important buildings, the Custom House and the Four Courts, without which the quays of Dublin would be so much poorer. Gandon had come to Ireland to design the Custom House, and Dawson, who had met him in London, commissioned him to design a great house in Laois to replace his old seat, Dawson Court.

In his early days in England, Gandon had been an assistant to Sir William Chambers, a prominent English architect whose great rival was Robert Adam, and Emo Court has close similarities with Adam's Shardeloes in Buckinghamshire, completed about 1769. Gandon's designs for Emo were not fully carried out, however, and as Dawson died during the 1798 rebellion, work did not continue until the north portico was added in the 1830s and the dome in 1860.

In the late nineteenth century when the Prince of Wales, later Edward VII, was looking for a house in Ireland, Emo Court was considered. The prince had stayed nearby with his friend, Lord Castletown, and knew County Laois very well. Winston Churchill also stayed here in the early twentieth century. The Portarlingtons left Emo in the 1920s, and in 1930 the house was sold to the Jesuit order, which ran a novitiate and a school there until 1969. During their tenure much of the fine statuary and at least one fireplace were removed because they displayed nude figures: some were stored in the basement, but locals say some were buried but no one knows where. In its heyday the house accommodated 600 priests and students, but by 1969 it had become quite rundown. It was the good fortune of County Laois, and the nation, that it was bought by C.D. Chomley-Harrison, who set to with purpose on extensive restoration works, employing lots of local people in the process. The statuary that could be found and the fireplaces removed by the Jesuits were put back in place, and several of Gandon's ideas that were omitted originally, such as the three-dimensional (*trompe l'oeil*) designs painted on the ceilings of the entrance hall, were implemented and the house returned to its former splendour.

It is worthwhile taking a walk around the outside of the house before having a look inside. It is quite an austere building, but on close examination there are exquisite details to be found. I was particularly impressed by the large plaque, made from Coade Stone (a kind of terracotta), above the north door showing an intricate classical scene, and two others, at the top of the south-facing end blocks, showing cherubs engaged in artistic activities, including reading architects' plans.

At time of writing (mid-2005) Mr Chomley-Harrison still lives at Emo and therefore only a limited number of rooms are open to the public. The entrance hall leads into a wonderful rotunda under the great coffered dome: this space was used by the Jesuits as a chapel and the inlaid hardwood floor was damaged by the insertion of an altar. It has been restored, however, and is the finest example of inlaid work that I can recall in Ireland, in fact, it reminds me of similar work in the Ducal Palace in Urbino, in Italy. Look out for the fireplace in the drawing room, a riot of marble cherubs and bunches of grapes, which was found in pieces in the basement and restored to its former glory. What I particularly liked was the 'lived-in' feeling of the house: the pictures, the family portraits, the ornaments and the little normal touches, such as the cluster of *aperitif* bottles and glasses on a table, which clearly are frequently in use, and also the lack of those red ropes you find in other houses to keep you away from the furniture. I also liked the variety of rooms—from expansive and gloriously decorated reception rooms to small, cosy 'withdrawing' rooms in relaxing, subdued colours. It is intended in future to open more of the house to the public, and locals tell me that the kitchens, in particular, with their arrays of Victorian equipment, pots and pans, are fascinating. Unfortunately, at the time of writing there is no descriptive brochure of the house available.

Opening hours for the house are: June–September, Tuesday–Sunday, 10.30am–6.30pm; closed on Mondays. Admission: €2.75.

There are 100 acres at Emo Court, which are in the charge of the State: the formal gardens surrounding the house consist of sweeping formal lawns and terraces, statuary and tree-lined walks. Beyond is an extensive informal landscape, originally laid out by the inventor of the 'natural' garden, William Robinson, and featuring woods, meadows and the lake. Most of the garden should be accessible by wheelchairs, and the many circuits of pathways are very popular with local people taking their constitutional. A simple photocopied map that can be obtained at the house shows a series of walks: particularly worthwhile are the Beech Walk, which will take you east to a plantation of Handkerchief trees, a spectacularly beautiful variety introduced from China in the nineteenth century, the Clucker Walk, which is ablaze with azaleas and rhododendrons in early summer, and the Lake Walk, which, although not fully completed at time of writing, takes you down to the shore of the charming, wood-embraced lake.

When leaving the Emo estate, if you would like to see another example of Gandon's work and the only rural church designed by him in Ireland, it is worthwhile making your way to nearby Coolbanagher church. Go straight across the main street of the village and continue to the next T-junction, where you turn left. Coolbanagher church is on the left after 600m. Externally it is a rather plain building with half-round Diocletian windows and a tall, slender spire that is a later addition, but the interior is special, and far superior to that of other churches of the period. If the church is not open, it may be possible to get a key from the old rectory next door (you can enquire at Emo Court). The side-walls are lined with niches and decorated with Roman motifs, such as swags and medallions. The niches were left empty in Gandon's time, but Mr Chomley-Harrison, so keen to complete Gandon's work in his own house, donated the substantial Roman urns to fill them. The place has survived as it was in Gandon's time with the exception of the ceiling and the apse (at the altar end of the church), which were added later, and, I suppose, the pews: in Gandon's time the gentry would have occupied pews with solid walls. An interior view attributed to James Malton hangs at the back of the church and shows it as it was then. Also at the back of the church is a rare medieval baptismal font.

The church is built on a slight eminence, but due to the lack of high ground for miles around there are fine views in clear weather north and east to the Wicklow Mountains.

To return to Dublin, go back to the village of Emo and turn right. The road runs along the demesne wall of Emo for less than 2km (1.2 miles) until it reaches the New Inn roundabout. Turn left, passing the Gandon Inn, and go right at the next roundabout to reach the M7 for the return journey.

TOUR 13

Kildare town, the National Stud and the Japanese Gardens

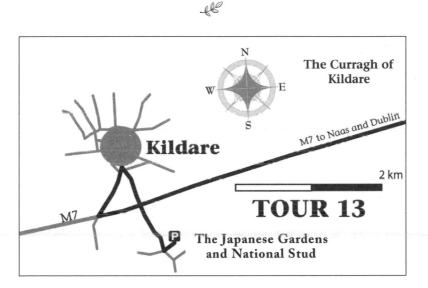

Kildare town grew out of an important early Christian settlement founded by St Brigid about AD 490, and it has one of the two round towers in Ireland that you can climb. For those who like animals, or have an interest in horse-racing, the National Stud is a must, and right next to it are the unique Japanese Gardens.

ROUTE: The N7 and M7 are taken to Kildare, and the return to Dublin is by the same route.

DISTANCE: 92km (58 miles).

MAPS: OS Discovery numbers 50 and mainly 55.

Take intersection 9 (the Red Cow) from the M50 and head south along the N7, more commonly known as the Naas Road, Ireland's first long dual carriageway, passing some fine modern buildings in the outer suburbs of Dublin, including Independent Newspapers printing facility, designed to show off the industrial process of printing.

The M7 motorway is joined nearly 22km (14 miles) from the M50 exit, and followed south-westwards to the town of Kildare, bypassing Newbridge. Just before reaching Kildare town the motorway crosses the Curragh, an open, hedgeless plain of some 5,000 acres, which, outside of mountain moorland, is the largest unenclosed area in Ireland. There is evidence of ancient Irish occupation on these plains as far back as the Stone Age. Within sight of their camp on the Hill of Allen, it was here, according to legend, that Finn Mac Cumhaill and the Fianna, ancient Ireland's standing army, practised their equine and military skills. In pre-Christian times it was an important place of assembly, and even that far back it was renowned for its horse races; the annals mention the High King of Ireland taking four chariots to the 'Curragh of the Races' in the first century AD. The landscape provided good sources of spring water and good drainage and was therefore an ideal place to house large armies, and by the sixteenth century it had become normal for armies to camp here for long periods. The main military camp in Ireland, the Curragh Camp, was officially established on the Curragh in 1855.

Over to the right you will see the stands of the Curragh Racecourse, where the tradition of horse races continues to this day, while to the left some of the buildings of the Curragh Camp can be seen over the trees.

Take Exit 11 from the motorway, and follow the R445 into Kildare town.

Kildare town is a very historic place (Kildare, Cill Doire in Gaelic, means the Church of the Oakwood, or Oak tree). It seems that it was an important ritual centre in pre-Christian times and was absorbed into the Christian culture when a monastery was founded here in the late fifth century by St Brigid, who may originally have been a pagan priestess before becoming Christianised. Women played an important part in the early Irish Church, and Brigid is perhaps the best-known. She was a popular saint in the Celtic world, and many of her followers became missionaries in Cornwall, Wales and Scotland: you will find

Kilbrides in Scotland and numerous Llansanffraids (the Church of St Bride) in Wales. Her 'mantle' is still revered to this day in Bruges Cathedral, where it has been since the late eleventh century.

Within a century of its foundation the monastery at Kildare had become very wealthy and was a residence of the Kings of Leinster, but the town and the monastery had a turbulent history. The monastic settlement was razed to the ground in AD 770, suggesting that most of the buildings, if not all, were of timber construction. In AD 830 the monastery was attacked by the neighbouring Irish and many monks were killed, and five years later the place was again sacked, this time by the Danes. There followed three centuries of frequent attacks and burnings: in the eleventh century alone, Kildare was destroyed five times.

A perpetual fire, probably a throwback to the pagan era, was kept alight in the monastery from the time its foundation, a tradition that still survived when Giraldus Cambrensis, secretary to the Anglo-Norman Prince John, paid a visit at the end of the twelfth century. It was briefly extinguished by Henry de Londres, the Anglo-Norman Archbishop of Dublin, in 1220 and apparently only finally ceased to burn at the dissolution of the monasteries in 1540.

The Heritage Centre and Tourist Office occupy the old market house in the central Market Square. Here you can see a permanent exhibition of the history of the town in audio-visual format, and also a large-scale model of the area as it was in early Christian times.

Behind the Silken Thomas pub on Dublin Street are the remains of one of the most important Norman castles in Leinster, the thirteenth-century Kildare Castle—one of the principal seats of the powerful FitzGerald family. It was occupied up until the mid-twentieth century, and the 1798 patriot Lord Edward FitzGerald, who was shot dead in a skirmish prior to the Rebellion, lived in a lodge beside the castle.

At the west end of the Market Square, in the highest part of the town, you will find St Brigid's Cathedral and the round tower, open to visitors May–October, weekends 10.00am–1.00pm and 2.00pm–5.00pm, and Sundays 2.00pm–5.00pm. The cathedral was badly damaged in the wars of the 1640s, and towards the end of the nineteenth century was nothing more than a roofless ruin. What you see today is the result of substantial rebuilding and restoration works, which were completed in 1896.

The building houses an interesting collection of fragments, curiosities and surviving monuments from the old cathedral and these are well worth exploring. Just inside the door is the fine Gothic tomb of Bishop Wellesley, who died in 1539, with the recumbent stone-carved effigy of the bishop, in full regalia, depicted on top. You could spend a lot of time interpreting the many images carved on the tomb: the sides and ends are intricately carved with a crucifixion scene (see how many of the instruments of Christ's Passion you can identify, i.e. the three nails, the seamless garment, etc.) and the figures of various saints, including St Patrick, St Peter and St Thaddeus, who is carrying a club. Look under the top slab, at the left corner of the end nearest the door, for a surprise—a Sheela-na-gig, a grotesque female fertility symbol.

Behind a screen opposite the entrance door I found another medieval carved stone, called the Indulgence Stone. It depicts St Michael weighing souls, a figure in armour, and the crucifixion, with angels collecting the blood flowing from Christ's wounds.

Another tomb to note is that of Maurice FitzGerald, who was a member of that most important Kildare family. His effigy is dressed in Italian armour-plate of the sixteenth century: note the chained monkey, the family mascot, on the pillow.

Outside the building, features worth noting and amusing for children, particularly, are the stone-carved gargoyles that drain the roof parapet, representing bishops, farmers, etc.

The round tower near the cathedral is one of only two in Ireland that are open to the public, as far as I am aware; the other being St Canice's Cathedral in Kilkenny. Round towers of this sort are almost entirely unique to Ireland, and acted as the belfries of early Christian churches. They were also used as watch-towers and for the temporary safe-keeping of books and altarware in times of attack, and for this reason the door was placed out of reach—in this case, 5m above ground level. St Brigid's round tower is over 32m high, and a wooden stairway has been installed. The tower you see today represents two stages of construction. The bottom half is built from granite, and probably dates from the seventh or eighth century. This original tower may have been damaged and the top part rebuilt, in limestone, in the twelfth century. The usual conical roof was replaced by a battlemented parapet in the eighteenth century, and from here there is a marvellous view over the surrounding countryside and the town. Admission to the tower is €3 for adults, €1.50 for children.

After visiting Kildare town, drive south from the Market Square (you came in from the west) and keep on straight, going left at a Y-junction and passing over the M7. After a short distance you will reach the townland of Tully and pass by the 'business' entrance to the National Stud, behind the gates of which stand the ruins of the Black Abbey, built by the Knights Templars in 1212. Tully is the ancestral home of the Sarsfield family, the most famous member of which was Patrick Sarsfield, Earl of Lucan and Jacobite general. Take the next turn left to reach the Japanese Gardens and National Stud visitors' car park.

Entry to the Japanese Gardens and the National Stud costs €8.50 for adults, €4.50 for children, €6.50 for students and OAPs, and a family ticket is €18. Opening hours are 9.30am–6.00pm, seven days a week, from 12 February to 12 November.

The stud farm, covering 320 hectares, was established by Colonel Hall-Walker at the end of the nineteenth century. The colonel was a wonderful eccentric whose belief in astrology led him to construct the stabling for stallions and mares ('Boxes' in horsey parlance) with rooflights, so that the stars could exert magical influences on the animals. He did indeed have considerable success with the horses he bred, and became rich enough to present the whole stud farm to the British Government in 1915 so that a national stud could be established. For his efforts he was created Lord Wavertree. In 1943 the farm was handed over to the Irish State and became the Irish National Stud.

Those unfamiliar with horse-rearing will no doubt be surprised by the comparative luxury of the conditions in which the horses are kept here, and by the highly organised way in which the stallions and the mares are encouraged to procreate winning progeny. But it is, perhaps, not surprising once you consider that many of the horses are valued in figures that ordinary souls would only use playing Monopoly, and therefore have to be looked after very well indeed. The thoroughbred horse industry is a huge one in Ireland and earns large export income, and centre of this industry is the National Stud. There is an excellent museum of the history of the horse in Ireland, stretching back 4,000 years, which includes the macabre skeleton of the champion, *Arkle*, whose disappearance at the height of his career and subsequent death remain a mystery. For adults and children alike, however, the high point of the visit to the stud must be the opportunity to admire the horses, mares, stallions and foals, at relatively close-quarters, as they graze in their paddocks.

Another gift that has been handed down by the eccentric Colonel Hall-Walker is the Japanese Gardens. In Edwardian times, oriental, and particularly Japanese, gardens were all the rage and the Colonel hired a well-known Japanese gardener, Tassa Eida, and his son, Minoru, to help him reclaim a small bog here and create a garden. Unlike many other such gardens which have disappeared, this Japanese garden, with its oriental trees and shrubs, rocks and water features, has been carefully nurtured for the past 100 years and is a great joy to behold. It can be enjoyed on many levels: you can follow the signposted 'Path of Life' through the garden from Birth to Death, finishing at the Gateway to Eternity, or you can simply wander about aimlessly, absorbing a unique visual and aromatic treat.

Nearby, as a millennium project, a new garden has been established, designed by Martin Hallinan and dedicated to St Fiachra. St Fiachra was an Irish monk who travelled widely in Britain and on the Continent. He became a hermit in the Forest of Breuil in France, and founded a monastery there in the seventh century, where he became a great horticulturalist. He is the patron saint of gardeners, and also probably of taxi-drivers: in AD 1640 hackney carriages, which used to have a stand outside the St Fiachra Hotel in Paris, became known as 'Fiacres', and they still are.

The garden is entered through a stone-lined tunnel that delivers you into a place of ponds, woodlands and running water. Overlooking a small lake rests a bronze sculpture of St Fiachra, seated on a limestone slab, while the centrepiece of the garden is a re-creation of an early Christian hermitage, in which there is a subterranean garden of handmade Waterford Crystal rocks, orchids and ferns glittering in the subdued light.

Altogether the National Stud and the two gardens (including four acres of woodland walks) can provide hours of family entertainment. There is a picnic area in the car park, or, if you prefer, a good restaurant (named the Wavertree) where full meals are served. There is also a craft shop where books, knitwear, pottery and Irish National Stud branded goods may be purchased. Almost all areas are wheelchair accessible.

Return to Dublin the way you came, via the M7 to the M50.

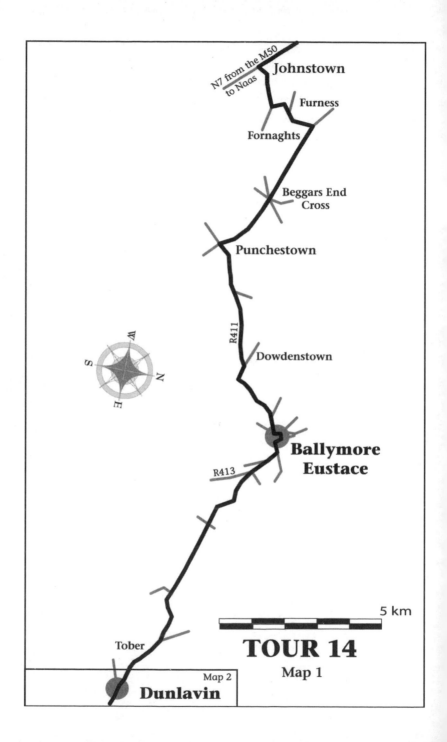

TOUR 14

Map 1

TOUR 14

Ballitore village and Moone High Cross

The historic village of Ballitore dates from the late seventeenth century and it became an early centre for the Society of Friends, also called the Quakers, who first held a meeting here in 1707. The ruined sixth-century Columban monastery of Moone is the site of St Columba's Cross, one of Ireland's finest High Crosses.

ROUTE: **Exiting the M50 at the Red Cow Roundabout (intersection 9), the route heads south towards Naas, turning off the main road at the village of Johnstown and continuing via Rathmore, Ballymore Eustace and Dunlavin to Ballitore and Moone. As an alternative, you can take the slightly shorter, but faster and more direct route to Ballitore by the Naas Road and Kilcullen bypass motorway. The return journey is by the N9, the M7 and N7.**

DISTANCE: **112km (70 miles).**

MAPS: **OS Discovery numbers 50, 56 and 55.**

At 20km (16 miles) from the Red Cow exit, turn left off the Naas Road into Johnstown, an historic, pretty village on the old coach-road to Dublin. It has a very large and well-laid-out garden and conservatory centre. Opposite the Johnstown Inn, a coaching inn established in the late seventeenth century, is the ruined medieval church of St John the Baptist, which has some interesting tombs of the Flatesburys and Wogans, one-time landlords in this area, and a Celtic cross commemorating Richard, Sixth Earl of Mayo, who was Governor of India at the time of his assassination in 1872. His body was brought back from India preserved in rum, much to the horror of the canal men who, as was their custom, had tapped the barrel for a small libation on the voyage up the Barrow before realising what else it contained.

Leave the village by the road opposite the garden centre, and after 250m take the left fork. Keep on straight for 1km (0.6 mile), and turn right at a T-junction. The stone wall to the left encloses the Furness Demesne: just before the next junction, 700m on, you can stop for a good view of Furness House in the distance.

Furness House is a fine example of the 'chunkyness' of early Georgian architecture. It was built about 1840 for Richard Neville, MP and was possibly designed by the amateur architect Francis Bindon. Just over the demesne wall is a tall monumental column surmounted by the figure of *Mars*, a twenty-first birthday present given in 1962 to Mr David Synnott by his father, the then owner. The column came from Dangan Castle, County Meath, the boyhood home of the Duke of Wellington.

Keep on straight at the junction, passing the Fornaghts House Demesne on the right. Fornaghts was the home of the Wolfe family from about 1750 to 1980. The family had many famous members, both English and Irish, including General James Wolfe, who fought at Culloden and was responsible for the capture of Quebec, at which engagement he was fatally wounded. Another famous Wolfe was the Rev. Charles Wolfe, who wrote the poem 'The Burial of Sir John Moore'. Theobald Wolfe Tone, the revolutionary leader, was the son of the Wolfes' coachmaker at Blackhall, near Clane, and was given the name Wolfe in honour of the family.

Turn right at the next T-junction and continue 2.5km (1.5 miles) to Beggars End Crossroads and continue straight through. Punchestown Racecourse is on the left, while on the right, past the main gates to the racecourse, you can catch a glimpse of the Long Stone—at 7m tall, one of the tallest prehistoric standing stones in Ireland. At the next crossroads turn left for the R411.

After 1.5km (1 mile) you pass the gates of the Dublin Gliding Club. Visitors are welcome, and children will not be alone in finding the whole process of glider flight fascinating: the gliders are towed into the air by a powered aircraft, and at the end of their flight gracefully and silently arch down to land. Subject to wind and weather conditions, and at a reasonable cost, a flight in a two-seater glider can be arranged for those interested in taking up the sport, or simply for the thrill of the experience, which I highly recommend. (For further details: Dublin Gliding Club, Gowran Grange Airfield, Naas, County Kildare.)

About 1.5km (1 mile) further on, at Dowdenstown, look out to the left for a great motte, a grass-covered mound that during the early stages of the Norman conquest would have been fortified with a timber pallisade fort.

The town of Ballymore Eustace ('the large town of the Eustaces') was originally established here, on the River Liffey, in the early Norman period to protect a forded river-crossing. Near the bridge stand the ruins of a mill in which 700 people were employed in the early 1800s, producing woven goods. In St John's Church of Ireland a monument to one of the FitzEustace family is worth visiting. Dating from the sixteenth century, it depicts a knight dressed in chainmail and helmet lying with his head on a pillow and his feet on a dog. The Catholic church in the town is of late eighteenth-century date.

Driving south out of Ballymore Eustace and crossing the six-arched stone bridge, take the first turn right, and after 1km (0.6 mile), take the second of two roads to the left. After 5km (3 miles) you reach the R756. Turn right and note the rolling, decayed parkland of the old Tober Demesne to the right, at one time owned by the Anglo-Norman family, the Tyntes.

Look out on the left for the old graveyard of Tober. If you would like to take a break from driving, there is space near the gate to park awhile and explore this ancient site. Tober, meaning 'well', was settled early in the Norman period, possibly on the site of an earlier fortification, the mound and terraces of which can still be discerned. Children can search for the oldest tombstone in the graveyard: there are quite a few dating from the eighteenth century, and I am told there is also an ogham stone, although I couldn't find it. Nearby are the ruins of Tober House, built in 1720, and although the front elevation shows a relaxed attitude to symmetry, a fine 'shouldered' doorcase was included to show an awareness of the fashions of the period. Even in its ruined condition it is possible to see that the house was given an extra storey later in its life. Nearby are the ruins of a watermill. In the laneway just above the graveyard is an exquisite example of a late eighteenth-century wrought-iron gate, a rare survival in this age of tractors and farm machinery.

A little over 2km (1.2 miles) beyond Tober is the town of Dunlavin, a really pleasant early eighteenth-century market town. In the centre is a spectacular, granite-domed Market House of 1743, perhaps the finest structure of its type you will find in Ireland. Built by the landlord Tynte family, it cost all of £1,200, a small fortune in its day. Apart from fulfilling its duties as a market house, it served as a place of safety for loyalist families of the area in 1798 when it was fortified with a garrison for their protection, and it also served as a gallows when four rebels were hanged from the pediment between the columns in May 1798.

Turning right at the top of the town drive south for just over 3km (1.8 miles) and turn right again to pass through Colbinstown; there is an interesting ancient graveyard called Killeen Cormac in the fields to the left, 700m from the bridge over the River Griese. In that graveyard, between two pillar stones, one marked by the paw-print of a magical hound, you will find the grave of King Cormac of Munster, plus some other ancient standing stones, the base plinth of a High Cross, ogham stones and an unusual slab depicting the crucifixion scene.

At Colbinstown you pass into County Kildare. Keep on straight and after less than 3km (1.8 miles) you will reach the N9, the main Dublin–Waterford road. Turn left onto the main road and within a couple of kilometers watch out for a sign for Ballitore, and turn right.

The village of Ballitore was founded by two English Quakers about 1685, and was the first planned Quaker village in either England or Ireland. The village became a battleground during the 1798 Rebellion, the gory details of which were recorded by a resident, Mary Leadbetter, in her journal, and later published under the title *The Annals of Ballitore*. Although some of the old houses are in ruins, there is a special quality about the place, and if the restoration works that have been carried out in recent years are continued, it could become a tourism centre of considerable importance.

A short walk north-west of the village brings you to Crookstown Mill. Built in 1840 and powered by the River Griese, it has been restored in recent years and you can see how flour-milling was traditionally done. The ship's steering wheel that controls the sluice gate comes from an old canal barge that was wrecked in the nearby Barrow Canal.

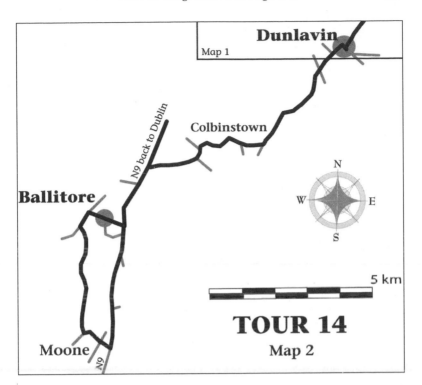

Abraham Shackleton founded a school just west of the village in the eighteenth-century; unfortunately the building has disappeared, but the location is marked by a plaque. Pupils included such illustrious personages as the great orator and parliamentarian Edmund Burke, Henry Grattan, Napper Tandy and Paul Cullen, who became a controversial Archbishop of Dublin and the first Irish Cardinal. Ernest Shackleton (1874–1922), Arctic explorer, was a descendant of Abraham and was born in nearby Kilkea House.

To the south is the original Quaker Meeting House of Ballitore, which, after being used as a store for many years, was rescued from virtual ruination and restored so well that it won a European Heritage award in 1979. It is now in use once more as a house of prayer.

Well worth a visit for refreshments is The Harp Bar, an old-world pub opposite the ruined markethouse. The actor Gabriel Byrne, who has family members in the area, has frequented the place over the years.

In the centre of the village is Mary Leadbetter's house: it dates from

Mary Leadbetter's house, Ballitore

the eighteenth century and has been carefully restored as the Ballitore Museum. Mary Leadbetter was Abraham Shackleton's grand-daughter and the village post-mistress, and she lived here for many years. She was a prolific writer and poet, published her first book in 1794 and kept a diary from the age of fourteen. The diary chronicles life in the village from 1766 to 1824, and in its published form, as *The Annals of Ballitore*, has become a valuable social history source. The museum displays a number of artefacts related to village life, and includes a fine display of nineteenth-century dress and lacework, including a wedding dress of the early 1800s, said to be the first garment to be sown by machine in Ireland. Facilities include a children's library/playroom, and a very pleasant paved garden with picnic tables and a sandpit for children. Storytelling for children is also offered by the centre.

Nearby is the Shaker Store, and even if you can resist buying, the showroom is well worth visiting just to see the range and quality of furniture, toys and woodwork available, and to take elevenses coffee or tea with delicious cakes and tarts. For younger children, there is an outdoor playground overlooked from the showrooms/café.

~—

Leaving Ballitore, head west to a T-junction and turn left. After a short distance, bear left at a well-restored little cottage and in just under 3km (1.7 miles) you reach the ruins of Moone Abbey. There is room for a few cars to park at the entrance.

The 5m-high Moone High Cross, which I think is the most beautiful of all the Irish High Crosses, stands within the ruined walls of the Abbey. It dates from the ninth century, and one of the reasons for its good state of preservation is the fact that it was buried during the Cromwellian period to protect it from destruction. At the end of the 1800s it was rediscovered by the Kildare Archaeological Society and reassembled. Dúchas (now Department of the Environment) has erected explanatory signboards dealing with the history of the cross and the meaning of the rich assembly of biblical scenes it displays, such as the temptation of Adam and Eve and the sacrifice of Isaac. Children will easily identify the twelve apostles and the Flight into Egypt, but can they find the dolphin? Nearby are the remains of another cross, perforated by a hole and decorated with depictions of animals and human-like creatures. This cross, and particularly the hole through it, is seen as a direct link with pre-Christian perforated fertility stones.

Behind the ruined Abbey stands a fine Palladian house called Moone Abbey House, with sweeps connecting the main house to two wings with unusual curvilinear gables. Opposite, just past a pretty old gatelodge with diamond-paned windows, are the ruins of an old mill building; note the fine iron-work gates with the monogram 'M' incorporated into the design.

Carry on to the main road, passing between the great gates that were originally the gates to Belan House, an eighteenth-century house designed by Richard Castle (architect of Leinster House), but now in ruins. In the fields around can be found a rotunda temple and two obelisks that were associated with the house.

At the main road turn left to return to Dublin via the N9 and intersection 9 (Red Cow Roundabout) on the M50.

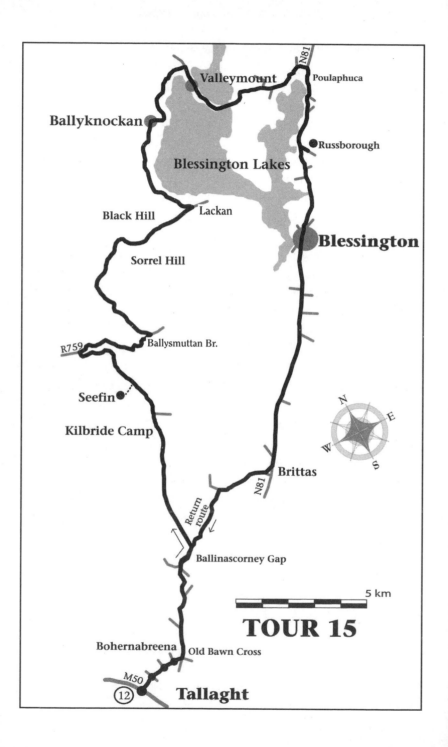

Valleymount

N81

Poulaphuca

Ballyknockan

Russborough

Blessington Lakes

Black Hill   Lackan

Blessington

Sorrel Hill

Ballysmuttan Br.

R759

N
W   E
S

Seefin

Kilbride Camp

Brittas

N81

Return route

Ballinascorney Gap

5 km

TOUR 15

Bohernabreena   Old Bawn Cross

M50

(12)   Tallaght

Wicklow Hills and Lakes

~🌿~

This tour takes you on a scenic journey into the hills, where a brief but steep climb will take you to a mini-Newgrange passage grave, and then on to the Wicklow Lake District and, via an old granite quarrying village, to one of Ireland's finest Palladian houses.

ROUTE: Side roads, some no more than metalled *bohereens*, are followed into the hills to circle the Blessington Lakes, and then on to Russborough via the N81 and back to Dublin the same way, via the N81 and Blessington.

DISTANCE: 75km (47 miles).

MAPS: OS Discovery numbers 50 and mainly 51.

Leave the M50 at intersection 12 (Ballyboden). Cross to the west side of the M50 and go straight through the roundabout, following a sign for Firhouse and the Ballycullen Road. Go through three roundabouts, and at the next traffic lights, at Old Bawn Cross, turn left onto the R114, following signs for Bohernabreena and Ballinascorney. Within minutes the Dublin Mountains loom up ahead as the road heads south into Bohernabreena, where it crosses the River Dodder by a narrow bridge. On the left is the entrance to the Rathmines and Rathgar Reservoir, constructed in the 1880s to supply clean water to the expanding suburbs of Dublin City, while at the same time ensuring the continuation of a good supply of water to the forty-five mills strung out along the River Dodder at the time.

The road now begins to climb towards the Ballinascorney Gap, a deep ravine between Killinarden Hill and Slievenabawnoge, on the left passing a turn for Glenasmole, one of the legendary hunting grounds of

Finn McCumhaill and his Fianna. As the road begins to level out, go left at a fork, up a narrow side road, passing a large but simple stone cross on the right, said to have been erected in the early 1800s in memory of a man who was killed here when a hayrick overturned.

This road is one of the highest passes through the Dublin Mountains, reaching its highest point of 460m a little less than 1km (0.6 mile) from the summit of Seehan Mountain (648m), just over 8km (5 miles) from the M50, before it begins to descend to cross into County Wicklow. As the road emerges from forestry the great cirque of Kilbride is revealed ahead to the left, sweeping slopes of bog and heather surrounded by the rounded summits of Seehan, Corrig, Seefingan and Seefin Mountains. Most of the area under the mountains here is owned by the Department of Defence and used by the Army as a shooting range.

Shortly after passing the entrance to Kilbride Camp on the left, you pass a turn for Blessington on the right before the road ascends again. Take note of the mileage at this junction, and less than 2km (1.1 miles) further on, look out on the left for a gap between the trees that goes straight up the mountainside. There is a grassy patch at the bottom of the gap where you can park. On top of the mountain above, Seefin, there is a passage grave that is well worth a visit. Although it shouldn't be attempted in bad weather or poor visibility, on a clear day this climb, with due care, is well within the capabilities of healthy humans from seven to seventy. The ascent is about 360m, the distance up and back about 2.5km (1.5 miles), and if you take your time, with frequent breaks for breathers, it is very achievable and very rewarding.

Climb straight to the top of the forest and continue on straight, alongside an old wall, through rocky, heathery ground, taking care with your footing. As the steep slope begins to lessen and there is a lot of rock coming through the peat, bear left, following an often muddy path up onto the summit of the hill. Just when you are wondering where the passage grave is, it appears ahead: a great cairn of stacked rocks.

This monument, 25m in diameter and 5m high, was built about 4,500 years ago, before the peat covering the mountains began to develop. The people who built it probably farmed this hill, which would have been easier to clear than the thickly forested, swampy lowlands.

Indeed, core samples taken from the bottom of the peat nearby contained plantain pollen, a good indicator of early agricultural activity and pointing to the fact that before the peat began to develop, you might have seen livestock grazing the grasslands and fields of crops. It seems probable that the people who farmed the hill lived in timber-framed houses around their cairn, much as modern villages surround a church. If anything now remains of them, it is at the bottom of the peat. There are about 300 passage graves of this sort surviving in Ireland, the most famous of which is Newgrange. If you look around you here on Seefin, you will see at least three other passage graves on nearby hilltops.

Entrance to the tomb on Seefin

The entrance to this tomb is on the north side of the cairn and if you are agile and reasonably slim, you can squeeze into it to reach the chamber at the end of the 5m-long passage: children will really enjoy the 'Temple of Doom' atmosphere of it. There is an easier way to get into the chamber, however. There was a collapse about 200 years ago, and during the archaeological excavations of the tomb in the 1930s the collapsed chamber was left open to the sky, so you can get in through the top of the cairn. Exposed to the damp air of the mountains, the rocks, with clusters of hart's tongue fern between them, are upholstered with rich green mosses, but the layout of the chamber, with its three burial niches, is easy to see.

After taking in the magnificent view from here, which extends from the upper Liffey around to the Blessington Lakes and beyond, descend again, with care in the rocky places, back to the car.

Continue downhill into the valley of the River Liffey and upon reaching the R759 Kilbride/Sallygap road, turn sharp right and follow it as it follows the Liffey westwards. As the road swings around towards the north-west, watch out for a side road signed for Blessington and turn left onto it. It takes you down to cross the young River Liffey by Ballysmuttan Bridge: there is an informal grassy layby here, where you can park a while and enjoy the scenery.

Continue steeply uphill through a hamlet of ruined, stone-walled cottages, and take the first turn to the left off the Blessington road. The road narrows as it climbs around the eastern slopes of Sorrel Hill, with fine views ahead towards Mullacleevaun, the second highest mountain in Wicklow, and to the left up the Liffey valley. The road is quite rough along here, so take your time and enjoy the views.

At 450m above sea level the highest point of the road is reached, and a great view of the Blessington Lakes opens up to the west and south. It is a relatively new view: before 1940 there were no lakes, just a valley where the Kings River and the River Liffey joined and together flowed on into County Kildare. In 1938 the people living in this valley were moved out to alternative locations: seventy-six farmhouses and labourers' cottages were demolished, all the trees were cut down and all the interments in the local graveyard were exhumed and re-buried in a new cemetery near Blessington. The Liffey was dammed at Poulaphuca and the valley began to fill with water: it took a few years to fill the new reservoir completely, to the extent you see today.

Follow the road downhill: in the valley on the left, after the abortive and bloody rebellion of 1798, many retreating Wicklow rebels camped here, hoping to hold out until the promised French invasion took place. There were as many as 1,000 men in the camp, including, for a time, leaders such as Michael Dwyer, a Catholic from the Glen of Imaal, and Colonel Holt, a Protestant from the Roundwood area. It was from here that the rebels consolidated their hold on the Wicklow highlands, raiding loyalist outposts and generally harassing Crown forces, until winter and weariness led to their gradual dispersal. Holt gave himself up in November 1798, but Dwyer held out until 1804. Both were transported to Australia.

In the little village of Lackan you turn sharp left at the local shop and continue downhill and southwards a few kilometres to reach the village of Ballyknockan. At the northern side of the village is a large stone slab with the legend 'Welcome to Ballyknockan Village' adorning a picnic layby, which has the finest picnic tables you are likely to see in Ireland, carved from local granite and given a highly polished finish.

Ballyknockan is a unique village, and it does not take long to realise why: it was built to house quarrymen to mine Wicklow granite, and almost everything you see is fashioned from granite, even things such as fenceposts, which elsewhere would have been made from some more prosaic material. Granite is used comprehensively in the buildings, from the most modest cottage to the larger houses, and it looks as if the stone-cutters could not resist decorating their work with lavish carved detail. Elements such as chimneys, window reveals, doorcases and gate piers—even on those buildings in ruin and not yet resurrected by the Celtic Tiger—display a richness of design not found elsewhere. It is worthwhile pausing here and taking a short circuit of the village on foot.

A couple of hundred metres after a sharp bend to the left and uphill, bear right at a fork down a narrow lane and then bear right again to reach the car park of the Ballyknockan Inn, one of the two pubs in the village. The doorway to the pub is a wonderful confection of granite: leave the car park and continue along the narrow and, as yet, unsurfaced lane. As you ascend the lane note the decorative window surrounds on the house on the left and the fine glimpses of the lake to the right.

Quarrying of stone began at Ballyknockan in the late 1820s and the stone was used in some of the large and earliest post-Penal laws churches in Dublin, such as those at Westland Row and Gardiner

Street. The *bothán̄s,* or huts, that would have originally housed the quarry workers and their families were replaced by the houses you see today when the quarrying became intensive and really lucrative in the 1850s and the population was a sizeable 450. The organic layout of the lanes and sites, however, remains the same, lending Ballyknockan much of the character it has today.

When you reach the tarmac 'main street', turn left and go right at the next junction. This takes you uphill a few hundred metres to see one of the finest houses in the village, appropriately named 'Granite House', which was once the Quarry Manager's residence. The road bears left and after a short distance bears right at Granite House. Opposite the gate lies a great granite millstone and a roughly shaped, unfinished statue of a lion. It is one of a 'pride' of lions cut for the entrance avenue to Stormont Castle in Belfast, but was rejected because it was a little smaller than the others. Granite House is the most formal house in the village and displays some beautiful granite details, such as the slender chimneys and the doorcase, which would not be out of place in a church.

Retrace your steps downhill again and turn right at the junction to continue. The village's second pub, Cullens', is passed on the left before you swing around to return to the Inn, passing by a cottage called St Anthony's that has a wealth of decorative detail in its stonework. There is much more to discover in this fine little village, and the suggested short circuit is intended to whet your appetite.

At time of writing (mid-2005), Ballyknockan is a slightly decayed place in the process of transition. However, the combination of the fine granite work, the informality of the network of lanes and its siting overlooking the lakes will ensure that it will be a much sought after location in the future, if due care is taken with ongoing improvements and development.

———

Leave Ballyknockan and continue south around the lake to reach a T-junction: turn right in the direction of Valleymount and Blessington. The village of Valleymount boasts a wealth of fine granite work, but it lacks the hillside informality of Ballyknockan. The church is a plain building of 1803, but has a later, most unusual façade and entrance gates comprised of stone pinnacles. Local lore suggests these were built by some quarrymen who had worked for a while in New Mexico and were inspired by what they saw there.

The road continues on to cross an inlet of the lake by bridge: there are car parks on both sides of the bridge, giving access to the lakeshore and an ideal picnic spot. On the western side of the bridge take an immediate left, and after less than 4km (2.4 miles) you will meet the N81 at a T-junction. Turn right, pass Poulaphuca House (where lunches are usually available) and cross Poulaphuca Bridge. The Gothic bridge, designed by the Scottish engineer Alexander Nimmo in the 1820s, spans the Liffey in one great arch, the keystone of which is 55m above the surface of the river as it cascades into a deep gorge after flowing out of the Blessington Lakes. It was the centrepiece of pleasure grounds laid out here around the same time by Lord Milltown of nearby Russborough, which included sheltered seats, grottoes, walks and a ballroom. It continued as an important beauty spot in Victorian times, but since the ESB built a dam and power station here in the 1940s it has not been possible to view the gorge, except from the grounds of Poulaphuca House.

At Poulaphuca the route passes briefly into County Kildare and then back into Wicklow, as fine views of the lakes and mountains beyond can be seen to the right. Less than 3km (1.7 miles) from Poulaphuca the classical façade of Russborough House can be seen across parkland on the left: shortly after, turn to the left to reach the triumphal arch that forms the great gate to the demesne.

Russborough is open to the public on Sundays and Bank Holidays in April and October, and every day from May to October, 10.00am–5.30pm. Visits are by guided tour only, and a tour of the main rooms costs €6 for adults and €3 for children. There is an additional charge of €3.50 per person to see the bedrooms.

Russborough was built in 1741 to the designs of Richard Castle for Joseph Leeson, who had inherited a large fortune at the age of thirty and who became Viscount Russborough in 1760 and Earl of Milltown in 1763. It remains one of the very few houses of the period that has survived almost unaltered, having all its original doorcases, inlaid floors and baroque plasterwork—probably unequalled elsewhere in Ireland. The Earl was a great collector and in Russborough he gathered together a very fine collection of paintings, statuary, furniture and silverware.

During the 1798 Rebellion the house was occupied first by the rebels, and then by government forces. The rebels were tempted to use the large green baize floor-covering in the saloon for making flags, but fortunately decided against it because they felt their hard-soled *brogues* might damage the floor. The government forces, on the other hand, caused serious damage to the building and to various works of art.

In 1929 the house and demesne was offered to the Irish Nation, but the generous offer was turned down. The house was bought in 1951 by Sir Alfred Beit, and he filled it with an exceptional assembly of fine art and *objets d'art* collected from the 1890s onward by his father, his uncle and himself. In addition, Beit tracked down and restored to Russborough many works of art that had been sold out of the house. After a number of robberies, however—one of the most famous by the notorious Dublin criminal, The General, most of the art collection was loaned to the National Art Gallery, where it can now be viewed.

The rooms on show are magnificent, and the furnishings, artwork and *objets d'art* from all over the world make up a unique collection. You do not need a particular interest or knowledge of such matters to appreciate the work of the Francini brothers, those prolific artists who seem to have worked on the plasterwork of every building of note in Ireland at the time. They were responsible for three ceilings, those in the music room, the saloon and the library, and it is not hard to see the comparison between these and the riotous plasterwork of the staircase hall, which is probably the work of an Irish stuccadore who was impressed by the Francinis' work but unable to control himself!

Another outstanding feature of the rooms are the mantelpieces and fire surrounds: by far I prefer delicate examples, such as that in the music room—a particularly beautiful panel depicting Leda and the Swan, the latter looking rather rough and masculine—to the rather monstrous and uncomfortable example in the library. I also like the mantle in the tapestry room, which beautifully illustrates Aesop's fable about the dog with the bone: the dog sees the reflection of his bone in the water and it looks bigger, so he drops what he has to get it … and ends up with none.

—∞—

Leaving Russborough, turn left again to head back towards Dublin on the N81. In less than 4km (2.4 miles) you encounter Blessington, a bustling and prosperous country town that suffers a little from heavy traffic. It was established in the 1670s by Archbishop Boyle of Dublin, who was granted extensive lands in the area as a reward for his service to the English Army during the rebellion of 1641. Boyle, a cousin of Richard Boyle, Earl of Cork, was a busy man: he was subsequently Archbishop of Armagh, Primate of all Ireland, a job he combined with being Lord Justice of Ireland on three occasions. In the late 1700s the town, with 15,000 acres, passed into the ownership of Lord Hillsborough of County Down, who was made the First Marquess of Downshire. Most of the houses along the main street owe their existence to the improvements brought to the town by the Downshires at that time and subsequently, but the oldest building is probably St Mary's Church on the main street, built by Boyle in 1683. Its bells, still in use, were cast in 1682, and the large clock on the tower dates to 1698, making it one of the oldest such clocks in the country. There is a number of restaurants and cafés on the main street that provide evening meals, or you could enjoy the ambience of the Downshire Hotel, where families have taken 'high tea' after outings for many decades.

Return towards Dublin on the N81: shortly after re-entering County Dublin, you reach the hamlet of Brittas, where you take the right turn for Ballinascorney, onto the R114. The road takes you back towards the Dublin Mountains again, the most prominent of which is Seehan, which you passed by earlier, with its passage grave clearly visible on the summit. Just over 2km (1.3 miles) beyond Brittas the road bears sharp right and uphill, and after a few minutes winds northwards over the Ballinascorney Gap and the City of Dublin and the Bay come into view ahead. The outgoing route is rejoined, before descending from the Gap. At the Old Bawn Cross, take the right turn signed for the M50, Ballycullen and Knocklyon, which brings you back to the M50.

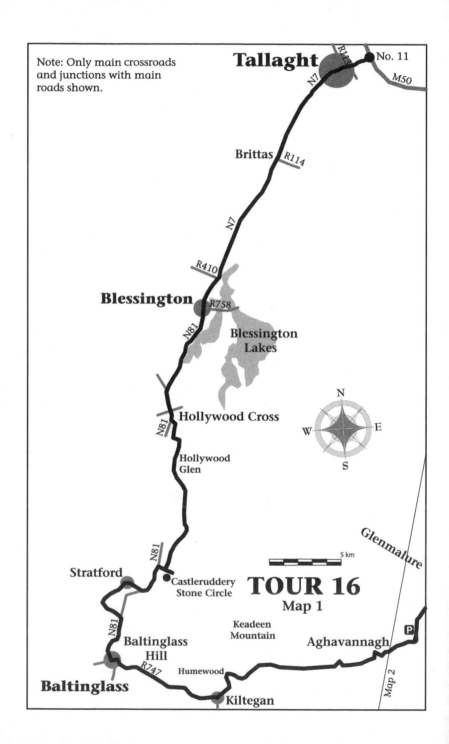

Note: Only main crossroads and junctions with main roads shown.

Tallaght

No. 11

M50

Brittas R114

N7

R410

Blessington R758

N81

Blessington Lakes

Hollywood Cross

Hollywood Glen

N81

N81

Stratford

Castleruddery Stone Circle

5 km

TOUR 16
Map 1

Keadeen Mountain

Glenmalure

P

N81

Baltinglass Hill

Aghavannagh

Baltinglass

R747

Humewood

Map 2

Kiltegan

A Circuit of the Wicklow Mountains

~~

This is a long and leisurely circuit of one of Ireland's most extensive mountain ranges, taking in a 4,000-year-old stone circle, an eighteenth-century 'boom-town', a medieval abbey, a farm museum, stupendous scenery and, for those who like a bit of exercise, a short climb that brings you up among the high peaks near Lugnaquillia. There is a lot to see and do, and more than enough to fill a long summer's day.

ROUTE: The N81 is followed south beyond Blessington and minor roads are used to circle around the south and east of the mountains to reach the Military Road (R115), before returning to the M50 via intersection 12 (Ballyboden).

DISTANCE: 167km (104 miles).

MAPS: OS Discovery numbers 50, 55 and mainly 56.

Take intersection 11 (Tallaght) off the M50 and head south on the N81 for Blessington, initially along the Tallaght Bypass that runs through the centre of Tallaght new town, which, hard as it is to believe, was a tiny rural village up until the 1970s. The built-up area is finally left behind as the road sweeps around to the left at the Embankment Lounge Bar, a name that derives from a nearby section of trench and earthen rampart built in medieval times to mark the boundary of the Norman-English Pale of Dublin.

The road now climbs briefly along the north-west foothills of the Dublin Mountains before passing a small lake on the left, called Brittas Pond, marking a distance of nearly 11km (7 miles) from the M50. Soon the north-western outliers of the Wicklow Mountains come into view lining the eastern horizon, before the route takes you through the small town of Blessington (about 20km (12.5 miles) from the M50), overlooked by its tall church clock tower that has been keeping the time since a few years after the Battle of the Boyne in 1690.

South of Blessington there are scenic glimpses of the Blessington Lakes to the left, with their panoramic backdrop courtesy of the Wicklow Mountains, and just over 25km (16 miles) from the M50 the route passes into County Kildare. It passes back into Wicklow after less than 2km (1.2 miles), and three more times in the space of 3km (1.8 miles) it slips into Kildare again, before finally settling into Wicklow. A little further on the route passes through Hollywood Crossroads, where there is a filling station on the left, and after less than 1km (0.6 mile), immediately after a sharp bend to the right, take the next turn left. This side road leads up into a landscape that is almost Alpine in character, Hollywood Glen, a 3km-long rift carved out of the rock by ice flows during the Ice Age. The Glen is less well-known than its more famous counterpart, The Scalp, near Enniskerry, but in my opinion it is much more impressive and has a beauty that surpasses that of The Scalp.

Emerging at the southern end of Hollywood Glen, the eastern horizon is filled with the broad sweep of Church Mountain, so called because of the ruins on its summit, which are thought to be those of a chapel constructed out of the stones of a prehistoric burial cairn.

A little more than 3km (1.9 miles) from Hollywood Glen is the pleasant and secluded village of Donard. Carry on straight through the village, which has a couple of good traditional pubs, and after less than 1km (0.6 mile) go right at a Y-junction. This part of west Wicklow is rich in historic and prehistoric sites, from Norman mottes to holy wells and from Megalithic tombs to stone circles, and the next stop is at one such site: the Castleruddery Stone Circle. At the next crossroads, about 3km (1.8 miles) on from the Y-junction, turn left towards the Glen of Imaal. The stone circle is easily accessible in a field to the left, 400m from the cross. You can park near the gate, but be sure not to block it.

Castleruddery Stone Circle, the largest of a number of similar sites in the area, consists of a circle of boulders surrounded by an earthen bank, with an entrance flanked by two great white quartz portals. The monument was probably used for ceremonial purposes in the late

Neolithic or early Bronze Age, the details of which are lost in the 4,500 winters the place has weathered since it was built. There is a remarkable feel of antiquity here and the collection of great boulders amidst a scatter of wizened fairy bushes clinging to the earthen bank adds to the sense of mystery. A description of the area given in the mid-nineteenth century suggests that locals still held on to the 'old faith': 'they got up early on Easter morning to see the sun dance, there was witchcraft, the Banshee wailed at Ballintruer, those ancient mounds and raths were haunts of fear, the hollows of old stones held magic water ... there was cock fighting, bull baiting and drunkenness.'

Go back to the crossroads and straight through to descend and reach the N81, and turn left. After 2km (1.2 miles) turn right off the main road, following a sign for Stratford. The River Slaney, which rises under Leinster's highest mountain, Lugnaquillia, and flows into the sea at far-off Wexford Harbour, is crossed before the road rises into what was, in the early nineteenth century, an industrial boom-town. At the time Ireland was experiencing a 'Golden Age'—not unlike the Celtic Tiger of recent years—and Stratford-upon-Slaney had a great future and the possibility of becoming a large, prosperous city.

Founded by the Second Earl of Stratford as a cotton production town, it was planned to have thirty streets, a church and a chapel arranged around nine squares, each with a fountain or an obelisk at its centre. Calico and cotton were produced, together with carpets, stockings, lace and ribbons; the bleach greens where the linens were laid out can still be seen today. The place survived the Act of Union in 1800, and by 1817 there were 500 workers employed in the town, which by then had a hospital, a school and places of worship for three religions. However, tariffs, taxes and newer methods of production in use elsewhere eventually brought an end to the cotton business here, and although attempts were made to diversify, they did not succeed. The population declined as people were forced to seek work elsewhere. The place gradually fell into disuse and was a ghost town by the end of the nineteenth century. By the second half of the twentieth century most of the fine streets and squares had disappeared into the rubble and dust. You can still, however, glimpse traces of what went before in the few surviving houses with Georgian doorcases, and a look into the graveyard of the pretty church at the top of the village will reveal tombstones with names such as Hanbidge, harking back to the many Scottish workers who came here to start the linen manufactory.

Leave the village following a sign for Rathbran cemetery, which brings you along narrow roads through a place called—for some reason long lost—Gibraltar. At a T-junction turn left and descend to pass Rathbran cemetery on the left. From the height of mound on which the graveyard stands, it would seem that it has ancient origins, although the earliest tombstones I could find dated from the mid-eighteenth century. The double-ringed earthen fort of Rathbran stood nearby up until the 1970s, when it was ploughed into the earth. From the annals this would appear to have been an important place, which at one time during the seventh century was the 'palace' of King Brandubh of Leinster.

Further down the hill the Slaney is crossed again and the route turns right onto the N81. A third crossing of the Slaney is made a short distance after, and 1.5km (1 mile) later you enter the town of Baltinglass. Turn left at the crossroads and cross over the Slaney once more to park in the town.

Baltinglass was probably originally established in the early years of the first millennium, on what was then an important ford over the River Slaney across which one of the ancient highways of Ireland passed, *An Bealach Conglais*, from which it gets its name. Nearby, on the ridge of Baltinglass Hill, are the eroded double banks and ditches of two spectacular earthen-banked forts called Rathcoran and Rathnagree. These are just two of five similar hilltop fortifications in the immediate Baltinglass area, including Spinan Hill, a massive enclosure encompassing 320 acres. In the Irish context such hillforts are thought, in some cases at least, to date to the late Bronze Age, about 1000 BC. On the summit of Baltinglass Hill and within the Rathcoran enclosure are the remains of a passage grave, but unfortunately it was partially destroyed by the archaeologists who excavated it in the 1940s.

The original settlement of Baltinglass got a new lease of life when a Cistercian Abbey was founded on the banks of the Slaney by Diarmuid MacMurrough, twelfth-century King of Leinster and infamous for his role in bringing about the Anglo-Norman invasion of Ireland. It was one of the first Cistercian establishments in Ireland, and within a few years of the monks' arrival in 1148 the wild landscape around had been transformed. Good arable land was cleared of trees and scrub and organised and diverse agricultural practices were established. The River Slaney was diverted and a great fish weir was built to harvest salmon and other fish using the latest European technology. By 1228, in addition to accommodation for the thirty-six monks and fifty lay brothers who were the standard backbone of Cistercian abbeys, a corn mill and woollen mill had been built to process the produce of the farm. By this time, too, it is likely that a small town would have grown up to house the Irish who were employed by the abbey, and their families.

After the dissolution of the monasteries in the sixteenth century the place swiftly fell into ruin, and in the ensuing centuries the stones of almost all of the monastic buildings were reused in the buildings of the later town, which was enlarged and improved by the Earl of Stratford in the late eighteenth century. He was one of the richest aristocrats in Ireland at that time: apart from owning Baltinglass and Stratford-upon-Avon, he inherited Belan House in County Kildare, Glenhammin in Suffolk, a mansion in Denmark Street, Dublin, and as if that wasn't sufficient he also built the fine Aldborough House in Dublin, although he probably never spent a night in it.

Today, only fragments of Baltinglass Abbey remain, and those only because a church was built within the main nave of the monastic church at the beginning of the nineteenth century. Located a few hundred metres north of the town near the riverbank, what remains of the Abbey is well worth a visit, in spite of its fragmentary nature. Accessed through the modern church grounds, a careful search of the remains of the original Abbey will be rewarded by the discovery of some very fine and typical Hiberno-Romanesque decorative stone carving. Note particularly the bases of the cut-stone corners of the main central crossing—where you will find sinuous floral and animal designs—the trimmings to the niches in the sanctuary area and the geometric designs, all different, on the capitals of the robust arcade columns. Rather unceremoniously shoe-horned into the ruin is the pyramidic mausoleum of the Stratford family, dating from the nineteenth century.

Near the Abbey the Slaney flows by gently: unfortunately, the picnic area established on the riverbank with tables and seats was a mess of litter when I passed by. Instead, if you would like a snack or a coffee, try a café called Relish, which you'll find on the corner of the west side of the bridge. The place is bright and cheery, spotlessly clean and they have freshly made paninis, bagels and strudels and very good coffee.

Baltinglass is a bustling country town, with two triangular 'squares' and, despite lots of new development, retains lots of original features. In the early 1950s it was the scene of the so-called Battle of Baltinglass, when the Department of Posts and Telegraphs appointed a new postmaster over the head of the popular local choice. Townspeople were incensed, the post office was boycotted and for a brief period the town was under siege—Garda reinforcements were needed, and even the Army was briefly involved, before the dispute was finally resolved; the local choice got the job.

Leave Baltinglass heading east by the R747 Kiltegan road. As you leave the town you get a final glimpse of the fort on top of Baltinglass Hill, up to the left. Further east, the great rounded shape of Keadeen Mountain, the south-east outlier of the high Wicklow Mountains range, rears into view before you reach the village of Kiltegan. Kiltegan is the estate village of Humewood, an estate that was in excess of 1,200 acres when taken over by William Hume in 1764. He was thought by his peers to be a liberal landlord, and during the 1798 rebellion some loyalists believed that the Humewood Yeomanry (a kind of local defence force) were actually United Irishmen and fighting on the other side. Towards the end of the rebellion, however, William Hume was killed in a skirmish with the rebels. As a measure of the regard in which the family was held, it was to Hume's son that the hero and arch-rebel Michael Dwyer finally gave himself up, at Humewood, in 1803.

Turn sharp left in the village and after a short distance, as the road bears right, you will pass the gates to Humewood, on the left. Unfortunately, the house cannot be seen from the road. It is an elaborate Victorian-Gothic pile, designed by architect William White, and completed in 1870 for the sum of £25,000—a full £10,000 over the original estimate—which was the cause of a long and expensive law case between the builder and the architect, which the builder eventually won. Today its owners insist it is not a hotel, but 'operates as a luxury private house' that is available to hire for conferences and corporate entertainment.

It can come as a surprise to some that this out-of-the-way area at the foot of the Wicklow Mountains could have been attractive to the well-to-do in the eighteenth and nineteenth centuries, but the land is actually very good here, and Humewood is only one of a number of large estates east of Baltinglass, quite of few of which are still intact and in private hands.

At the next crossroads, near a back-gate to the Humewood estate, turn right. Keadeen Mountain seems ever-present to the north along this stretch, but soon Lugnaquillia, the highest summit in Leinster and Ireland's highest mountain outside Kerry, begins to assert itself ahead and to the left. The road gradually climbs and after passing through the hamlet of Rathdangan, it leaves behind the field hedges and lush green fields of the lowlands. In their stead is a new landscape of stone walls, gorse and mountain bog, all overlooked by forested hills.

After crossing Carrignamweel Pass, at 320m above sea-level, a new vista opens up ahead: below is the scenic valley of Aghavannagh, backed by layer after layer of rounded mountains rolling out into the distance, towards the east. After crossing Aghavannagh bridge down in the valley you will be able to see the old military barracks, located on a height to the left. Built in the early 1800s to garrison the Military Road, which extends from here to Rathfarnham in south Dublin, the barracks was instrumental in bringing to an end the use of the Wicklow Mountains as a safe hideaway by Irish rebels. This particular barracks has served many purposes since: it was used as a hunting lodge by Charles Stewart Parnell and as a summer home by John Redmond, before becoming a youth hostel in the 1940s.

After passing through the hamlet of Aghavannagh, the route follows the old Military Road as it ascends the flanks of Slieve Maan, an eastern outlier of Lugnaquillia. At the highest point of the road, and the highest point of this route, 450m above sea level, you can park at a small car park to take in the vista all round. This is also your opportunity to briefly savour the experience of standing on one of the highest summits of

Wicklow, with the minimum of effort. To the east is Croghanmoira with its conical peak reaching to 664m above sea level. A rough track leads from the road beside the car park all the way to the top, a walk of just over 1.5km (1 mile), but a climb of 214m (700 feet), and I can promise a most rewarding arrival. From this unparalleled vantage point the views all round are superb, and if hillwalking is something you have not done before, the sense of achievement will be considerable. For those who want to do a little more, there is a narrow ridge extending first north-west and then north-eastwards from Croghanmoira, which ends in a dramatic viewpoint hanging over Glenmalure Valley. To do this and get back to the car will add 7km (just over 4 miles) and an additional ascent of about 100m to your walk. Be prudent, however, and do not take on these climbs if the visibility is poor, or the weather is deteriorating.

Continue downhill into Glenmalure, where another military barracks, this one ruined, is passed at Drumgoff before reaching a crossroads. To the left the road follows the Avonbeg river deep into the long glacial valley of Glenmalure. It was here that the Battle of Glenmalure was fought in 1580. The O'Byrne clan had their headquarters for centuries in Glenmalure, and the Brehon laws and customs and the Gaelic language survived here long after they had been abolished elsewhere in the east of Ireland by the English. The chief of the clan at the end of the sixteenth century, Fiach McHugh O'Byrne, held on fiercely to his territories, making frequent 'shopping trips' to The Pale for cattle, arms and the odd hostage. On one occasion, running short of lead shot for his stolen guns, he visited the village of Crumlin, south of Dublin, and made away with the entire lead roof from the church there. There was no route south through the mountains that the English could use to pursue him after his raids, so he was a constant scourge to the English establishment.

In August 1580 the newly appointed Lord Lieutenant of Ireland, Lord Grey de Winton, led a large force through Kildare and entered the mountains west of Glenmalure, hoping to surprise O'Byrne. It was a hot

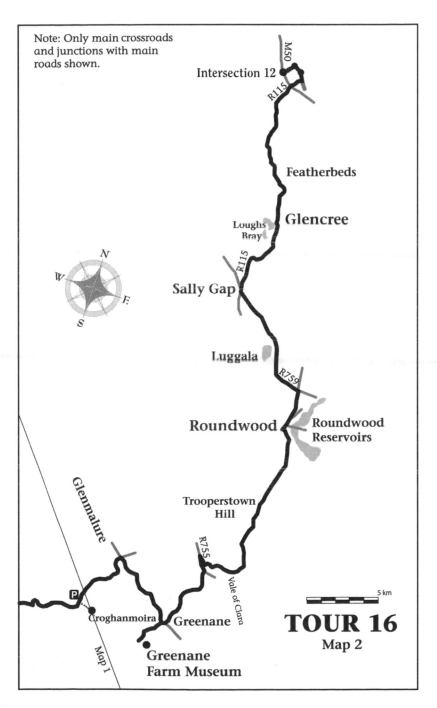

Note: Only main crossroads and junctions with main roads shown.

M50

Intersection 12

R115

Featherbeds

Glencree

Loughs Bray

R115

N
W
E
S

Sally Gap

Luggala

R759

Roundwood

Roundwood Reservoirs

Glenmalure

Trooperstown Hill

R755

P

Croghanmoira

Greenane

Vale of Clara

Map 1

Greenane Farm Museum

5 km

TOUR 16

Map 2

summer's day and the English were spotted early enough for O'Byrne to prepare a counterattack. As the colourful, and very visible, army under Lord Grey wound its way slowly along the bottom of the valley, the Irish on the heights above prepared the classic ambush: the English were somehow enticed to climb the valley sides, relinquishing the flat valley bottom for the steep, boulder-strewn incline. They were struggling up in this way when the Irish rose up from their hiding places and fell upon them, and slaughter ensued. Those still on the valley floor turned and fled; Lord Grey, his secretary the poet Edmund Spenser, and Walter Raleigh, one of his officers, escaped with about half their force, Grey being forced to abandon his caravan containing, among other belongings, his entire wardrobe! It was to be many years before government forces again ventured into the mountains in force.

Turn right at the cross: if you have taken up the challenge and climbed Croghanmoira, you can feel you've earned a stop at the Glenmalure Lodge just around the corner. They have been looking after mountain travellers here for more than 200 years. The English traveller Ann Plumptre, who came in 1815, was not impressed when kept waiting for two hours for a chicken lunch, but things had apparently improved a few years later when, in 1822, *Wright's Guide to Wicklow* describes it as 'a most comfortable inn'. Today it is a great place to stay if you are climbing or just relaxing in the quietude of Glenmalure, and is usually thronged with satisfied walkers on weekend afternoons.

The road meanders eastwards along the valley, with the Ballincor demesne to the right across the valley until, less than 6km (4 miles) from Drumgoff it reaches the hamlet of Greenane. If you have the time, you have the option of taking a short detour here to visit Greenane Farm Museum and Maze. Turn right and cross the bridge, then ascend the steep hill, after about 1.5km (1 mile) the Museum is on the left. (Opening hours: 10.00am–6.00pm, May–June, Tuesday–Sunday; July and August, seven days; September and October, Sunday only. Open all Bank Holiday Mondays. For information, visit the website: *www.greenanemaze.com*, or tel: 0404 46000.)

Greenane Farm Museum is a work of love by a father-and-son team, Jonathan and Will Wheeler. What is now an extensive venture began when Will, as a boy, began collecting old glass bottles. Soon he had piqued the interest of his father, an escapee from Dublin who had taken up sheep farming in Wicklow, and together they assembled a considerable collection, travelling around the county rummaging in the middens of old farmyards. As they did so, they also came across old farm machinery and artefacts that farmers were glad to be rid of; the age of the typical 'ethnic' Irish pub decor had not yet dawned, and there was no monetary value put on such things. In collecting all these items for the pure fun of it, they saved part of our heritage from the scrap merchants, and by putting them on display are helping young people of the computer generation to see into the past.

The more formal 'museum' displays are housed in a timber-sheeted barn and an old restored farmhouse. The farm museum is on two floors, and here you will find all the bits and pieces collected over the years by the Wheelers. Every type and size of saw you ever dreamed of is displayed here, together with old blacksmith and joinery tools, a wide variety of traditional *sleáns* for cutting turf and hand shears for shearing sheep, some old but very sophisticated horse-drawn farm machinery, much of it made from timber and each piece a wonder of engineering and craftsmanship, and one of the original weaving looms from the Avoca mills.

The kitchen in the old farmhouse has part of its original earth floor (the traditional three-legged stool of Irish cottages apparently came into being because of the unevenness of such earthen floors), and a wide fireplace—the engine room of the traditional cottage—with an array of pots and kettles hanging from a crane over the fire. Rough but functional tables and chairs, a settle bed and a dresser complete the room. In another room there is an impressive array of smoothing irons, butter pats, earthenware jam jars and other items that until recently were familiar parts of everyday rural life, but are now no longer to be seen.

Upstairs in glass cases is a collection of bottles, a fascinating assembly of glass containers from brown Virol bottles in all sizes and banana-shaped baby's bottles to ancient beer bottles and chemical containers from old chemists' shops.

All around the farm there are pigs and lambs and ducks and hens for urban children to enjoy. The nature walk is wonderfully unpretentious: the Wheelers have resisted putting in paved paths and handrails so you really feel you are wandering along the old *bohereens* of Ireland as you take a short circuit of the farm. Grassy paths bring you along overgrown hedges decorated with wildflowers, past little streams and ruined walls to a series of ponds where a timber causeway takes you out into a bog. Here, water hens, geese and herons can be spotted by quiet observers.

There are two mazes at Greenane, one of which is a recently laid out Solstice Maze: a simple astronomical observatory with twenty-one standing stones that Jonathan Wheeler says pre-school children like as much as the adults. The other maze is a more traditional one, where adults and children alike battle to find their way into the centre and out again via circuitous, confusing routes between dense walls of hedging; a nearby observation tower gives a very entertaining view of their navigation efforts.

Greenane Farm Museum has something for everyone, and is worth a separate visit.

———

Back at the hamlet of Greenane, on the north side of the bridge, continue past M.J. Byrne's old world pub and take the first turn to the left, signed for the Glenmalure Golf Club. The narrow road takes you uphill steeply again before descending into the Vale of Clara to meet the R755. Turn right and after a few hundred metres go left and steeply downhill to reach the Avonmore river and cross it by a narrow and ancient packhorse bridge. One of the oldest bridges in Wicklow, with six arches and just 3.25m wide, this structure dates from about 1680. A tiny church, dedicated to St Patrick and St Killian and built in 1799, sits picturesquely on the far bank. It is a beautiful and peaceful place to stop for a while: the broad, grassy riverbank between the church and the village has been landscaped informally and is an ideal place for picnics, or for just lying in the sun and being lulled to sleep by the soothing sounds of the water flowing by.

Continue steeply uphill again: go right at a Y-junction and less than 3km (1.7 miles) from the church turn left at a pretty gatelodge. The road meanders up through sheep country, the air filled with the bleating of lambs in late spring, and promenades along a hillside opposite

Trooperstown Hill. Keep on straight for the next 7km (4 miles), following signs for Roundwood at each junction you meet, and soon the Roundwood Reservoirs can be seen to the right before the road bends around into the village.

Roundwood is reputed to be the highest village in Ireland, and for some years it was the home of the second president of Ireland, Sean T. O'Kelly. Just east of the village are the reservoirs at Vartry Waterworks, which supply twelve million gallons a day to the householders of Dublin. This is your last chance to stop for refreshments before your return to Dublin, and there are plenty of suitable pubs and cafés to choose from.

Leaving Roundwood, our return is made along one of the most scenic roads in the north Wicklow area. Just outside the village take the left turn and less than 2.5km (1.5 miles) further on, turn left again onto the R759. A continuous climb takes you up 250m into a scenic mountainscape overlooking Lough Tay, a dark glacial lake in a deep valley. The horizon is lined with many Wicklow summits, a stratified typography fading into the distance. If it is a sunny evening, it is worth delaying just a little longer before returning to Dublin, and there is no better place than here. After reaching the highest point on this ancient road, the old name for which is the strange and ominous-sounding 'The Murdering Step', descend about 1km (0.5 mile) and park on the right in a small car park. You can cross the wall on the other side of the road and sit on the grassy slopes directly over the lake, with the cliffs of Luggala rising on the far side: a perfect place to watch the sun set.

Leaving this magical place behind, continue along the mountain road to reach the Sally Gap and Military Road and turn right. The return journey into Dublin follows in reverse the outgoing route described in Tour 17 (p. 153), past Kippure, the two Loughs Bray, and Glencree, to reach the Featherbeds and descend, via Killakee, to Ballyboden, re-connecting with the M50 at intersection 12 (Ballyboden).

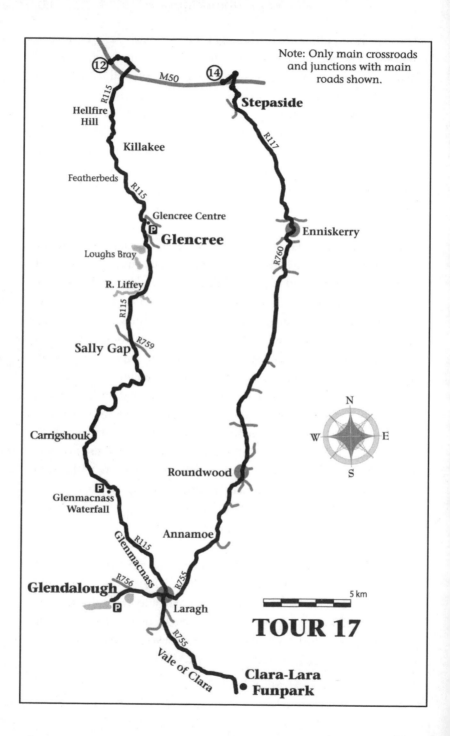

Note: Only main crossroads and junctions with main roads shown.

12

M50

14

R115

Stepaside

Hellfire Hill

Killakee

R117

Featherbeds

R115

Glencree Centre

P

Glencree

Enniskerry

Loughs Bray

R760

R. Liffey

R115

Sally Gap

R759

N

W   E

Carrigshouk

S

Roundwood

P

Glenmacnass Waterfall

Annamoe

R115

Glenmacnass

Glendalough

R756

R755

P

Laragh

5 km

R755

TOUR 17

Vale of Clara

Clara-Lara Funpark

Glendalough and Clara-Lara via the Military Road

لَهُ

G lendalough is one of the most beautifully scenic places not only in Wicklow but in Ireland. The mountain-enclosed valley with its two lakes was the site of a monastic settlement founded by St Kevin in the sixth century and there is much of interest to see there, including the remains of seven churches of the medieval period, a round tower and the ruins of a nineteenth-century mining village. Clara-Lara, on the other hand, is an extensive rustic funpark for children under twelve years. Depending on your preferences and needs, you could easily spend a full day in both of these places, particularly if you want full value for the entrance fee at Clara-Lara.

ROUTE: **From Rathfarnham in the southern suburbs, follow the Military Road over the scenic Dublin and Wicklow Mountains wilderness to reach the village of Laragh, beyond which is the Vale of Glendalough. Clara-Lara is 2.7km (1.7 miles) south of Laragh. The return journey is via the R755 and the quaint village of Annamoe, by Roundwood, Enniskerry, The Scalp and Stepaside, to rejoin the M50 at intersection 14 (Sandyford).**

DISTANCE: **86km (52 miles).**

MAPS: **OS Discovery numbers 50 and mainly 56.**

Leave the M50 at intersection 12 and head in the direction of Ballyboden. Four hundred metres from the M50, take the second exit off a roundabout. Continue to another roundabout and take the third exit and head south, turning right after 500m in the direction of the sign for 'The Sally Gap and Glencree'. The road climbs past wooded demesnes and Hellfire Hill, topped by an old hunting lodge where the Irish version of the Hellfire Club was said to have met, and comes out into the open at Killakee, where there are expansive views across Dublin City and Bay; indeed, in good visibility the Mountains of Mourne can be seen sweeping down to the sea 120km (75 miles) to the north in County Down.

Take the right fork at Killakee, and the road takes you out onto open heathery moorland surrounded by rounded summits, many topped with Stone Age passage graves. This road, known as Military Road, was built in the early 1800s to allow fast deployment of the Army into the Wicklow wilderness, which for so long had been the hideout of rebels and brigands. The road was, for its time, a considerable work of engineering, with 24km (15 miles) of its 77km (48 miles) length at over 370m above sea-level. The heather-clothed moorland here is called The Featherbeds, named for the seas of bog cotton that used to wave in the breeze here before most of the peat was harvested in the early twentieth century. A fine view opens up to the right: the long, deep valley of Glenasmole with two reservoir lakes glinting at its heart nestles below the rounded summits of Seehan and Corrig, which step up gently southwards towards the highest summit in the Dublin range, Kippure. Glenasmole is a place steeped in myth and legend, and ancient Irish sagas mention it as a favourite deer-hunting ground of Finn McCumhaill and his band of followers, the Fianna.

Almost all the mountains you can see from here are topped with prehistoric cairns and passage graves of the Neolithic period, and it is probable that early communities lived on all of these summits, their dwellings gathered around the great stone cairns like a village around a church.

After passing the 470m mark and crossing into County Wicklow, the road descends to pass by the valley of Glencree. In the thirteenth century Glencree was covered by a dense oakwood and was established as a royal deerpark. Eighty red deer were sent from the royal forest at Chester to stock the park, but the animals were frequently poached by the Wicklow Irish and the inhabitants of Dublin. Look out for a sign for the Glencree Centre for Reconciliation, originally a military barracks and subsequently a boys' Reformatory, now a place dedicated to

Old Barracks at Glencree

peace-building and reconciliation in Ireland and abroad. If you wish for a brief diversion, the first turn to the left since Killakee takes you down a few hundred metres to the Centre: there is an exhibition area and a coffee bar and they welcome visitors. Near the Centre, carved from a granite cliff-face, is the German War Cemetery, a peaceful, sylvan place through which a mountain stream rushes and where many members of the German forces of two World Wars are laid to rest. The graves include those of *Luftwaffe* aircrew who were killed in crashes, *Kriegsmarine* sailors whose bodies were washed up on Irish shores, and those of Herman Goertz and Oskar Metzke, German spies who landed in Ireland during the Second World War.

Back on the main route and 1km (0.6 mile) further on is a little cottage where the McGuirk family opened a tea house in the 1880s. It became a popular halting point for the occupants of coaches, charabancs and early touring cars, as well as for hillwalkers and cyclists, and remained in business through three generations until the 1960s. The tea house visitors' books, now preserved in the National Archives, provide a unique insight into the social history of the period and include the names of many who were involved in the political and cultural development of the new Irish State. Art collector Sir Hugh Lane, poet Austin Clarke, botanist Robert Lloyd Praeger and novelist L.A.G. Strong were among the visitors, while poet Denis Devlin contributed verses and Harry Kernof and Sean O'Sullivan are among those who left exquisite pencil sketches in the books. William Beckett, father of the writer and playwright Samuel Beckett, also features: he brought his son walking in the mountains many times and frequent references to the surrounding landscape appear in the playwright's work. Another playwright of note, John Millington Synge, boarded with the McGuirks one summer and while there wrote part of *In Wicklow: On The Road*, published in 1908.

A hundred and fifty metres behind the cottage, and accessible by a rough path, is Lower Lough Bray, one of two beautiful cliff-girded glacial lakes dominated by a dramatic promontory called Eagle's Crag Towers. Overlooking the waters, embowered in trees and rhododendrons, is a Swiss Cottage designed by William Morrison and erected in 1830, which has provided a retreat for many writers, including novelists Lee Dunne and Frederick Forsythe.

Our route now climbs steeply away from the cottage to pass by Upper Lough Bray, just 1km (0.6 mile) away in a heathery coum. Above the lake the road reaches a high moorland, and 2km (1.2 miles) further on the infant River Liffey is crossed at the beginning of its long journey west, north and then eastwards through Dublin City and into the Bay. James Joyce wrote in *Finnegans Wake* that the Liffey begins:

'on the spur of the hill in old Kippure, in birdsong and shearing time, but first of all, worst of all, the wiggly livvly, she sideslipped out by a gap ... while Sally her nurse was sound asleep ...'

The Sally mentioned here is the Sally Gap crossroads (named for the willow, or in Gaelic, *saileach,* wood that once stood here), an ancient east–west route from Kildare to east Wicklow, which you will cross 1.5km (1 mile) further on. Before reaching it, a long and broad view opens up to the west along the moorland valley of the Liffey. The scattered trees along the southern side of the valley are what remain of the Coronation Plantation, an ill fated attempt to afforest the area by the Marquess of Downshire, who named the plantation to celebrate the coronation of the Sailor King, William IV, in 1831.

Keep on straight at the Sally Gap as the road winds further into the Wicklow wilderness. For centuries these moors and the mountains of County Wicklow provided a safe base from which Gaelic clans could raid the civilised English of The Pale of Dublin, just 32km (20 miles) to the north. Wicklow continued to offer asylum to the rebel Irish long after the rest of the country had come under English law and order, and after the Irish Rebellion of 1798 some remnants of the rebel forces continued to carry out guerrilla attacks on English settlers from the safety of its hills. Early in 1800 the English authorities decided to take measures to ensure the mountains would no longer shelter rebels and brigands, and began by constructing a road from Dublin southwards through the mountain wilderness to Aghavannagh in County Wicklow. This new route would allow armies to be deployed quickly to any part of the county, and the road was to be fortified by the establishment of barracks every 16km (10 miles) along its length. Surveying for the road began in April 1800 and construction began in August, the work being carried out by Army engineers and sappers. The result of the undertaking, completed within seven years, was the pacification of the rebel county, and never again were the rebel Irish able to seek asylum in Wicklow. Military Road fell into disuse for the rest of the 1800s: it saw only local traffic and in places it was reclaimed by the creeping bog. In the twentieth century, however, an increase in touring to the beauty spots of Wicklow gave it a new purpose. Is it not strange how things turn out: this mountain road, built for warlike purposes, has today become a resort for peaceful commerce, leisure and enjoyment.

The road winds along contours between the rounded granite summits of the north Wicklow range, with long and beautiful views extending southwards. Passing a dramatic boulder-strewn outcrop of granite called Carrigshouk, the road climbs briefly onto yet another mountain-ringed plateau before descending near the great waterfall at Glenmacnass to reach cultivated land once again, and the village of Laragh, where a turn right will take you, after 2km (1.2 miles), to Glendalough.

This ancient religious site was established in the sixth century by St Kevin in a beautiful glacial valley that cuts deep into the Wicklow Mountains, enhanced by the two lakes that give the place its name. Seven churches are scattered across the valley, most of them gathered around a tall round tower within the old monastic enclosure, providing a window onto Ireland's past as the Island of Saints and Scholars. For nearly 500 years during the Dark Ages, when the roads to Rome and the Holy Land were either closed or unsafe, this monastery was an important place of pilgrimage in western Europe, and the antiquity of the place only becomes clear when you realise that it was at the peak of its importance 600 years ago. Of particular note is the monastery gatehouse, the only surviving example in Ireland, although it is difficult to view in context because of the souvenir stall erected in front of it. Monasteries were not subject to secular laws, and any fugitive who was allowed in through the gate was given sanctuary from the outside world. The monastic city was sacked and burnt on at least seventeen different occasions over the centuries, and not only by the Norsemen—the Irish of Dublin did their fair share of plundering here, too.

There is a good Interpretive Centre near the monastic site (tel: 0404

45325), which sells maps, guides, etc. and is open from mid-March to mid-October. The entrance fee to the display of models, photographs and a good audio-visual presentation dealing with the history and topography of the place is €2.50. While the peacefulness of the valley and the monastic site may be difficult to experience during the busy tourist season, there are two possibilities to get away from the crowds.

The first is a 2km (1.2 miles) there-and-back walk to St Saviour's Church. To do this, go down through the monastic buildings, past St Kevin's Kitchen (the building with the stone roof out of which a mini-round tower projects), out through a gate and across the river. Turn left and follow the path for 1km (0.6 mile—about fifteen minutes). Down to the left is St Saviour's, a substantially rebuilt ruin that has some of the most elaborate and exquisite stone carving of any of the Glendalough churches. Few people wander this far away from the centre, and you can usually dally here in peace. Children can search among the ornamental stone carvings for a lion biting his tail, and two birds holding up a human head!

The other way to get away from it all is to drive on past the hotel for 1km (0.6 mile) to reach the car park at the Upper Lake. The Upper Lake is the largest by far, and nestles between two great ice-carved cliffs. The lakeshore here and the valley to the west from here are my favourite parts of Glendalough. Gathered about on the eastern edge of the dark lake are fragments of early Christian crosses, a stone fort and a tiny, beautifully sited church, in the grounds of which early Irish Kings were buried. For those who like to walk and climb there are plenty of exciting options available from here on way-marked pathways described on maps available at the Interpretive Centre.

If you only want a short, level walk, I recommend you take the track up the west side of the lake to the ruined Miners' Village, a round trip of 4km (2.4 miles), about an hour and a quarter. Here the real isolation of the great valley, which attracted St Kevin to the place all those centuries ago, is easily appreciated. It is a place apart, a place of sheer cliffs and scree slopes, waterfalls and overgrown mine workings, inhabited by feral goats, peregrine falcons and ravens. For those who want to go on a little further, there is a prominent zigzag mule track leading up to a higher level, where among the heathers, bog cotton, ferns and bracken in this wild and wet landscape, lesser-known plants can be found, such as Ireland's two carnivorous species, the butterwort and the sundew, and where you may encounter herds of deer, or be lucky enough to sight a hare or a badger.

At the car park near the Upper Lake is a kiosk that sells snacks, drinks and ice creams. The Royal Hotel in Glendalough, just a few yards from the monastic site, provides lunches, snacks or bar-food at reasonable prices. Lynham's Hotel and the Wicklow Heather Restaurant in nearby Laragh also serve snacks or full meals.

To reach Clara-Lara, return to the village of Laragh, turn right onto the R755 and follow it south along the forested valley of the Avonmore River. Clara-Lara Funpark is on the left after 2.7km (1.7 miles). (Website: *www.claralara.com*; email: *dayout@claralara.com*, tel: 0404 46161.) Entrance fee for adults and children is Û8 each, but use of such attractions as the rowing boats, radio-controlled boats, etc. are extra. If you pay €16, children can get a 'gold bracelet' that gives them unlimited access to all rides. Children under four years and OAPs are not charged admission. The park is open from 30 April to 4 September inclusive, 10.00am–6.00pm. It is recommended that you bring 'old shoes' and a change of clothes!

Clara-Lara reminds me of the high-tech, water-based funparks one would find in the resorts of warmer countries, but its scenic setting along a flat, wooded valley straddling the Avonmore makes for a more rugged and natural environment in which children can enjoy themselves. The river is used to create the network of streams, waterfalls, ponds and small lakes that make the place so much fun. It is a wonderland of rope bridges, tall rope swings over ponds, boats and tree houses, one of which has three storeys, and moored in one of the small lakes is a pirate ship with decks, mast and rigging and below-deck compartments. There is no tiled swimming pool, but there are natural and safe swimming 'holes' that would appeal to Huckleberry Finn, and a very tall waterslide uses a gorse-covered hillside for its height.

For those children who are not fond of the water there is a mini-karting circuit where they can get the revs going, and for those who have tried everything else there is a miniature football pitch complete with goalposts, and a crazy golf course. Barbecue areas are provided for families who want to picnic in the park, but there is also a cafeteria that serves snacks.

There are no discouraging signs in Clara-Lara Funpark saying 'don't do this' or 'don't do that', and while every effort is made in the design and construction of the place to create a safe environment for vigorous physical activities, nothing seems over-protective: it all seems a very good place for energetic children to run wild and have great fun. I am told that most of the adults that accompany their children are as wet, as dirty and as happily exhausted as the children at the end of the day!

To return to Dublin, retrace your route to Laragh and continue on the R755, via Annamoe, Roundwood, Enniskerry and Stepaside to rejoin the M50 at intersection 14 (Sandyford).

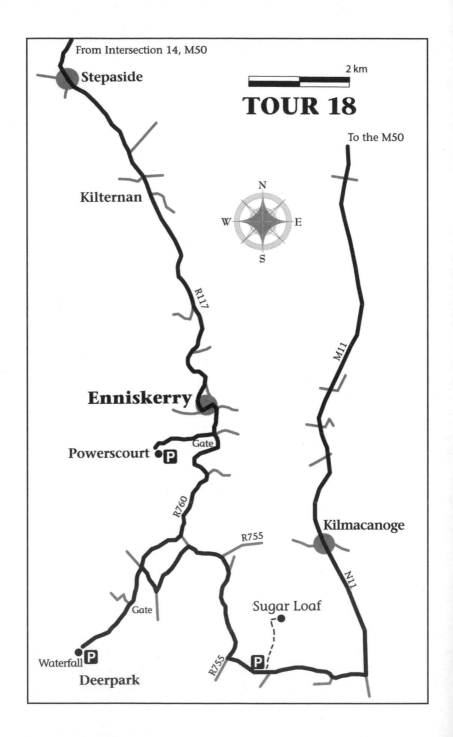

TOUR 18

Powerscourt Gardens and Great Sugar Loaf

P owerscourt Gardens are amongst the finest and most extensive
formal gardens in Ireland, incorporating fine statuary and
metalwork in a landscape of steep terraces and a wide variety of trees and
shrubs. Nearby is the scenic River Dargle and the dramatic 125m-high
Powerscourt Waterfall, which has been a tourist attraction for well over
200 years. For families with an adventurous streak, this tour includes a
visit to the Great Sugar Loaf, an inviting, volcano-like mountain that is
surprisingly easy to climb.

ROUTE: Leave the M50 at intersection 14 (Sandyford), and drive south
via Stepaside to Enniskerry and Powerscourt. Powerscourt Waterfall and
Great Sugar Loaf are reached by a series of side roads, and the return
journey is made via the N11 and M11 to rejoin the M50.

DISTANCE: 32km (20 miles).

MAPS: OS Discovery numbers 50 and 56.

Leave the M50 at intersection 14 (Sandyford) and take the exit off the
roundabout signed for the R113, Sandyford and Stepaside, crossing over
the motorway. Take the first turn off the roundabout on the south side
of the motorway. After a couple of hundred metres the cut-granite
gateway to Glencairn can be seen over to the left: this was formerly the
home of the colourful 'Boss' Croker, Corkman, US politician, New York
Fire commissioner and City Chamberlain, millionaire, Derby winner
and husband of a Cherokee Indian woman. Go left at the next
roundabout and follow a winding road to reach Stepaside village and the

R117 a little more than 2.75km (1.8 miles) from the motorway exit. Turn left and follow the road out through Golden Ball and Kilternan to reach The Scalp, 4.3km (2.7 miles) further on.

At The Scalp the road passes through a narrow, precipitous cleft in a granite hill. This deep gash, scattered with great blocks of granite, is a glacial spillway, where many millennia ago the dammed waters of a glacial lake to the north burst through to inundate the lands to the south. On the south side of The Scalp you cross into County Wicklow, and in moments the dramatic cone of Great Sugar Loaf appears ahead, and to its left the double domes of the Little Sugar Loaf.

Soon a winding, tree-lined road takes you past one of the first Gothic Revival churches in Ireland, designed by Patrick Byrne in 1842, and then down into Enniskerry, the scenic early nineteenth-century estate village of the Powerscourt demesne. Keep on straight through the crossroads above the centre of the village, following signs for Glendalough—look out for a fine little forge on the right with a horseshoe-shaped door—and when you reach a T-junction, turn right. The entrance gates to Powerscourt are at the top of the hill, on the right. The tariff for entering the estate and gardens is €6 per adult.

The avenue to Powerscourt House is bordered by neatly trimmed parkland and rows of mature beech trees with silver-grey trunks, between which, to the south, are breathtaking views of the countryside dominated by the cone of Great Sugar Loaf, which is never far away on this tour. You expect to be greeted by a full frontal view of the great house, so it comes as a surprise when you abruptly reach the great granite façade of the house, with its central block flanked by small wings and great arched classical gateways in curved curtain walls.

Powerscourt House was built by Richard Wingfield about 1740 from pale Wicklow granite quarried in Glencree; the name Powerscourt is derived from the de la Paors, a Norman family that came into possession of this mountainy land through marriage to a follower of Richard de Clare, or Strongbow. The centre block of the house was substantially gutted by fire in 1974, during which most of the original furnishings were also destroyed.

It has been refurbished since, but not as it was: it is now a visitors' and conference centre and as such the interiors represent little of what was before. The gardens, however, are as magnificent as ever. The centrepiece of the gardens consists of a broad terrace and a vast, 12m-wide staircase leading down from the south elevation of the house to a great circular pond. This formal base is surrounded by an extensive informal arboretum designed after eighteenth-century Chinese principles, which were concerned with bringing the distant countryside right up to the edge of the formal garden. Viewed from the terrace that is decorated with fine sculptures and with the Sugar Loaf as the backdrop, the whole is spectacular and cannot fail to impress, even those least interested in gardens or scenery.

There is a free map available that allows you to arrange your own tour of the garden, and there are many routes you can take; below I recommend aspects of the gardens that you should not miss. The formal parts of the gardens are wheelchair-friendly.

Surrounding the formal gardens is a plantation, including a wide range of exotic conifers, many planted in the mid-1800s, including a row of Giant Sequoias standing between the Italian Garden and the Walled Garden. These trees are native to the Sierra Nevada Mountains in California, and one of the species is the tallest tree in the world, a 116m giant. These great trees were only identified about 1850, but within a decade almost every large garden in Europe had some. As their timber is of no value and they are rarely blown down or destroyed by fire (feel their highly insulative bark, designed to resist forest fires), they tend to live for as many as 2,000 years.

There is a Pets' Cemetery at the south-east end of the gardens, which consists of over twenty tombstones laid out on terraces. Here lie family pets such as the dogs Little Botts, Modger and Jack, favourite horses and hunters, and even Eugenie, a champion cow who died in 1967 aged seventeen years. Eugenie had seventeen calves and gave over 100,000 gallons of milk during her lifetime.

Below the Pets' Cemetery is the Rhododendron Garden, which is not very extensive but a must-see in late May and June.

The Japanese Garden, down in a hollow to the east, was established in 1908. Although there is not really much that is Japanese about it other than the atmosphere, the fairytale entry to it from the direction of the lake will be very much to the liking of children: you are taken down a narrow, winding path and stairway under arches built from eroded limestone arches, all quiet but for the tinkling of a canalised stream flowing into a central pond full of giant water lilies.

The Pepperpot Tower is another feature that young children will enjoy. Its lower battlements are ringed with an interesting collection of old cannon guns, and for once here is a tower that children can safely climb and that gives good views over the gardens from the top.

For those interested in sculpture there is much at Powerscourt to enjoy: it is as much a classical sculpture park as a garden or arboretum. The main pieces are associated with the terrace, walled gardens and the formal staircase, and of particular note are the two figures representing the god of the winds, *Aeolus*, which you'll find at the pond under the centre of the terrace and which were originally made in the early nineteenth century for the Italian Duke of Arese.

Powerscourt House, as mentioned, was badly damaged by fire and has been substantially altered internally, the interior now containing an extensive range of shops selling everything from books and CDs to designer clothes and foodstuffs. Beyond the outhouses, opposite the car park, is a large, glazed garden centre.

For lunch, you have a number of options. You can stay in Powerscourt and eat in the cafeteria overlooking the gardens. There is an interesting range of dishes, but I found the prices quite expensive. Another option is to leave Powerscourt and drive a few hundred metres downhill into the village of Enniskerry, where there are a few good lunch options, including Poppies Restaurant. If you have come prepared with a picnic, there are two excellent possibilities. The first is within the Powerscourt demesne: drive out of the car park and turn right, following signs for picnic spots by the river. The road takes you downhill through the woods. When you meet a T-junction, turn right, and after a few hundred metres you'll find places to park and some idyllic picnic spots beside the

River Dargle, particularly when the rhododendrons are in bloom. The other option is to continue on with this tour and have your picnic in the Powerscourt deerpark, near the great waterfall.

To reach the deerpark, leave the Powerscourt demesne, turn right at the main gate and follow the road southwards. As you descend the hill half-a-mile further on, the grounds behind the wall to the left are that of Tinnehinch House. Tinnehinch was originally an inn, but was presented as a residence to Henry Grattan, orator and statesman, by the Irish Parliament in recognition of the part he played in obtaining parliamentary freedom from British control in 1782.

Crossing a narrow bridge shortly after, turn right (keeping on the main road), and nearly 1.6km (1 mile) further on, turn right again, following a sign for the waterfall. In a little over 1.6km (1 mile), you will reach the gates to the southern section of the Powerscourt demesne, which lead into the deerpark and waterfall. The admission is €4 per adult; children under two are free, while older children are €3 each.

You can park in the car park or drive on a little further and park on grass nearer the falls. There is a very good playground for children and a shop selling guides, sweets, ices and sandwiches. Downstream from the waterfall the Dargle meanders along ponderously, and it is safe for young children to paddle and play about the rocks supervised by their parents, who can sit contentedly on the grassy banks.

Powerscourt Waterfall is the highest in Ireland—some claim the highest in the British Isles. It is created by the River Dargle cascading down 123m from Glensoulan Valley into the cirque of the Powerscourt deerpark. The deerpark can be a busy gathering place for families in the summertime, but during the week, and particularly early in the day, you may have the place much to yourself. It is hard not to stand a while beneath the rockface and contemplate the waters that pour down thunderously. In wintertime the floods from above sluice down through a mass of great icicles. When George IV visited Ireland in the summer of 1824 he was entertained at Powerscourt, and he expressed interest in seeing the waterfall, which for the previous fifty years had been a tourist attraction. It had been a dry summer and the flow was weak, so a dam was placed on the river at high level to be released when the king arrived, ensuring he saw the falls at their most spectacular. To this end, a viewing bridge was erected across the river for the king and his party. The king had to leave Powerscourt early, however, and missed the show. When the dam was broken, the waters thundered over and washed the viewing bridge clean away!

There is a forty-five-minute, figure-of-eight pathway for those who want to stroll around the valley; a guide is sold at the shop and costs €1.

For the final location of the day, leave the deerpark, retracing your route from the gates uphill to the first crossroads, where you turn right. At the next junction turn left. This brings you down to meet the R760 at a T-junction; turn right, and after 900m take the side road to the right to reach, after 120m, the R755. Turn right and continue for 2km (1.2 miles) before taking a turn to the left; the Great Sugar Loaf car park is on the left after 700m.

Great Sugar Loaf is perhaps the most-climbed mountain in Ireland, and with a little energy and care the ascent is achievable in less than an hour by anyone between eight and eighty, in reasonable health.

A track leads towards the mountain: although the summit is over 500m above sea level, you have already driven most of that to get here, so the challenge before you is much reduced. There remains but 210 vertical metres and a little more than 1km (0.6 mile) between you and the spectacular pinnacle summit.

Follow the grassy path that climbs gently at first and then more steeply to reach the western side of the cone-like top. The path now turns east and heads straight up: the going is rough in places over the loose scree, and near the top you may need to use your hands, but the distance is short and in no time you will have conquered Sugar Loaf and be standing on the tiny, rugged summit. The views are quite wonderful, east to the Irish Sea, and west into the heart of the Wicklow Mountains; if you have the ordnance map, it is fun to try to identify all other locations in between.

Retrace your steps to get back to the car park; care should be taken on the descent, which is often as slow as climbing but uses different muscles. If you haven't done this climb before, it is a most worthwhile adventure, and you will not be able to drive past this Wicklow summit again without thinking delightedly, 'I was up there!'

To return to Dublin, leave the car park and turn left, and drive 2km (1.2 miles) to the N11, where you turn left again for Dublin and the M50, via the M11.

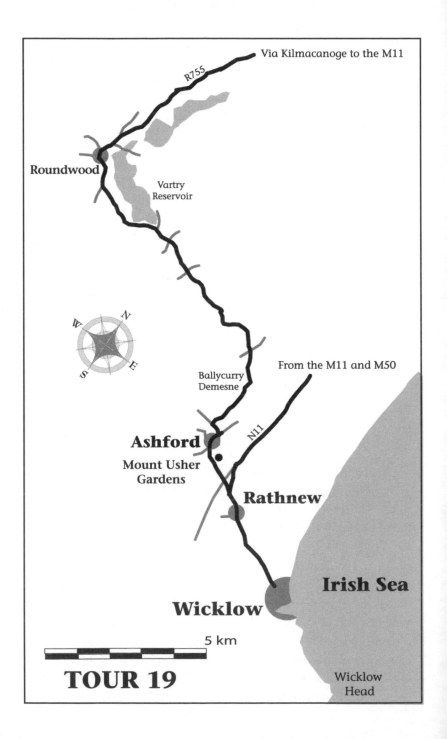

Via Kilmacanoge to the M11

R755

Roundwood

Vartry
Reservoir

N
W *E*
S

Ballycurry
Demesne

From the M11 and M50

N11

Ashford

Mount Usher
Gardens

Rathnew

Irish Sea

Wicklow

5 km

TOUR 19

Wicklow
Head

Wicklow Town and old gaol and Mount Usher Gardens

ɬɕ

Wicklow town is a pleasant place on the east coast that grew up around a sheltered harbour and a Norman Castle. The old gaol in the town has been restored recently and is a popular attraction for visitors, particularly children. The twenty acres of Mount Usher Gardens is one of the best examples in Ireland of the romantic Robinsonian garden style.

ROUTE: The M11 and N11 will take you directly to Wicklow town. The return journey is made via Ashford, Roundwood and Kilmacanoge to rejoin the M50.

DISTANCE: 80km (50 miles).

MAPS: OS Discovery numbers 50 and mainly 56.

Follow the M50 east and south to the M11 and N11. Continue on past the turn-off signed for Ashford, Mount Usher and Wicklow, which is about 23.3km (14.6 miles) out, and take the turn for Rathnew, Rathdrum and Wicklow, about 27km (16.5 miles) out, following signs for Wicklow. Other than in the outskirts, parking in Wicklow town is all by pay-and-display tickets, which you can buy at newsagents. The car park behind the Tourist Office in William Square (which is actually a triangle) is a useful base for exploring the town. The Tourist Office is a good first port of call and can provide maps and information on what is currently on in Wicklow. The centrepiece of William Square is a monument commemorating a son of Wicklow, Captain Robert Halpin of the iron-clad ship *Great Eastern*, which he commanded during the laying of the first successful transatlantic cable in 1869. He is praised for 'his many estimable qualities, and in proud remembrance of the distinguished services he rendered telegraphy in all parts of the world'.

Halpin is part of Wicklow's long maritime heritage; the tiny harbour here is the only haven along 40km (25 miles) of this coast between Greystones and Arklow, and would have attracted landings and settlements from the earliest times. Palladius—a bishop sent from Britain by Pope Celestine to evangelise the Irish before the arrival of St Patrick in AD 432—is said to have landed here and built three churches. St Patrick is also said to have landed here and to have been sent on his way again by the local ruler. In the eighth century the Vikings arrived and established a winter settlement in the estuary of the Vartry River, which became the nucleus of the town we see today. Three centuries later the Normans, under Maurice Fitzgerald, arrived and occupied the settlement, building the Black Castle to control the harbour. In later centuries, as a centre of English power, the town attracted the unwelcome attentions of warlike Wicklow clans, such as the O'Byrnes and the O'Tooles, and it was attacked frequently. In 1580 the castle and town were razed to the ground by Fiach McHugh O'Byrne. The town's isolation from the protection of The Pale meant the Gaelic clans at one time exacted 'protection money', called the Black Rents, from its English citizens. Although picturesquely sited, all that remains of the castle today is a few vestiges of walls clinging to the sea-cliffs east of the modern town. Today Wicklow is a pleasant, walkable, bustling place of colourful houses and interesting shops located on a hillside above the harbour.

Off the Market Square you will find Wicklow Gaol, once threatened with demolition but thankfully refurbished recently to become one of Wicklow's most popular tourist attractions (Website: *www.wicklowshistoricgaol.com*; tel: 0404 61599). Admission is €6, with concessions for OAPs and children; wheelchair access is very limited. There is a shop selling crafts and books and a café serving hot meals, sandwiches and beverages, and you can take your food out to picnic tables in the exercise yard of the gaol!

The gaol was built in 1702, principally to house prisoners convicted under the Penal laws, but in and after 1798 it was, of course, crammed with captured rebels. It was also used as a collection point for men, women and children sentenced to be transported to Botany Bay, mostly for what we today would consider minor misdemeanours, such as stealing a loaf of bread or an item of clothing. The place developed a fearful reputation for the harshness of its regime; horrendous overcrowding in extremely unsanitary conditions frequently led to the early deaths of inmates.

Today's visitors to the gaol are brought back in time through the building's history. There are guided tours led by actors dressed as gaolers, and self-guided tours of the cells with the aid of good audio-visual presentations, which tell the story of the gaol and individual prisoners. It was in use as a gaol up until the early twentieth century, and you will find graffiti left by recent prisoners scratched or carved into the simple wooden shelf-beds. One particularly sad note was left by a James Doyle of Bray, who tells us that he was sentenced for six months in 1878 by Lord Meath, whom he describes as 'an old hoor, bastard, ophel, God damn him'.

A large section of the display is devoted to the period when many prisoners were held here temporarily until they could be shipped to Van Diemen's Land, and describes the lives of the transportees and the strange conditions and surroundings they encountered in Australia. Famous Australians who are descendants of transportees are listed, including Paul Keating, who was Prime Minister between 1991 and 1996. A particularly impressive presentation is the partially recreated 'coffin ship', the *Hercules*, where you will be met on deck by the captain in full regalia to the sound of splashing water and creaking rigging, and shown below decks to hear the passengers' stories.

It is an educational and a child-friendly place, if a bit macabre, with some simple interactive displays that children will enjoy. A mock prisoner release form, stamped and dated, is issued to all leaving the gaol.

North of the town, and accessible just across the bridge a couple of minutes from William Square, is a 4km-long spit of land called the Murrough, formed between the sea and a lagoon called Broad Lough, which is fed by Leitrim River. It was once commonland for grazing, and in the nineteenth century it was the location of a Cholera House, where victims of the disease were kept isolated from those on the 'mainland'. The southern end became industrialised in the twentieth century, but the remote northern end is a wonderfully fragrant place of clovers and herbs and wildflowers attended upon by hosts of bees and butterflies. An informal nature trail has been laid out along the Murrough, skirting around the unsightly industrial estate and taking you out to the marram grasslands to the north. Poppies are particularly spectacular here, their vibrant, blazing discs of red standing out from the midst of the other colours that, in contrast, pale to insignificance. The Murrough is one of the few places in Ireland where you can see both hen harriers and marsh harriers in one place. If you are very lucky, you might catch sight of ospreys, which often spend a time here on their spring migration to their Scottish breeding grounds, and can be seen swooping down and using their talons to pluck unsuspecting mullet from the water of the lagoon.

Less than 400m walk from the centre of town, appropriately up Church Street, St Thomas' Church of Ireland church stands in a quiet northern suburb and is worth a visit. Built in 1700 on the site of an earlier church, it was improved in 1777 with the addition of a four-storey robust clock tower sporting an unusual, copper-clad cupola similar in shape to an Eastern 'onion' dome. Note the weather-vane atop the dome: it is in the shape of a lion bearing a sheaf of straw, the crest of the Eaton family who paid for the improvement works of 1777. There is a twelfth-century Romanesque doorway reconstructed in the porch, which is possibly taken from the old, pre-eighteenth-century church.

The churchyard has a large number of slate tombstones, on which the lettering is as sharp as the day it was cut. The earliest stone I found was dated 1696, but there are many from the early eighteenth century. Billy Byrne of Ballymanus, executed in 1798 and commemorated in the 1798 monument in Market Square, is buried here.

The centrepiece in the graveyard is a great Egyptian-style funeral urn in white marble, dating from 1768, with an inscription to Benjamin Wooley of Surrey on one side, and on the other an inscription to the Rev. Robert Truell of Clonmannan, who died in 1830. Look for the stone to Thomas Wilson, who died in November 1791, which bears the inscription:

> Remember me as you pass by,
> As you are now so once was I;
> As I now am, so you must be.
> Then prepare to follow me.

For lunch, if you have brought a picnic, you have a number of choices. You could have it on the Murrough—particularly pleasant in the late spring or early summer when the wildflowers are at their perfumed best—or you could have it at Black Castle, where you may sight seals offshore. If you drive or walk south along the coast for a few kilometres, you will reach Wicklow Head, the easternmost point in the Irish Republic, where you will find no fewer than three lighthouses. A winding track leads out to the head; in early summer it winds through a grassy sward thick with bluebells, seapinks and stitchwort. The oldest lighthouse, an octagonal granite tower built in 1781, is now for rent as a holiday home. A smaller, circular lighthouse stands nearby, closer to the sea, and a third one, still in use, can be found downhill below the head, where it was placed because the older ones were obscured in foggy weather. Here there is also an opportunity to watch seals cavort offshore, and to see kittiwakes on their nests.

The Bakery Café in Church Street, well-known in Wicklow for evening meals, also serves good lunches, but if you have time, you could wait until the next stop on our route, Mount Usher Gardens, where there is a cafeteria.

Depart Wicklow and return through Rathnew, heading for Ashford and Mount Usher Gardens. The motorway is crossed and less than 2km (1.2 miles) from Rathnew, just before entering Ashford village, watch out for Mount Usher Gardens on the right. Visibility is poor on the bend, so take care with your right turn into the car park. The entrance charge is €6, with concessions for OAPs and groups, etc. There is a cafeteria and a little cluster of boutiques (which include a pottery shop, a country clothes shop and a second-hand bookshop) that have little to do with gardens but make for interesting browsing. The ideal times for visiting the gardens are May and October, when you get the best of the pretty late spring flowering and the riotous autumn colours.

Picnics and dogs (and paper bags) are not allowed, and although the gardens are accessible for pushchairs and wheelchairs, the rusticity of some of the paths can make it hard going.

Mount Usher Gardens were established by Edward Walpole in the

1860s. Like many Victorians he enjoyed country walking, particularly in County Wicklow, where he encountered and became friendly with the owner of Mount Usher Mills, eventually acquiring the property. Utilising the waters of the millrace and pond, he established the gardens here, which were later improved and extended by his sons in the Robinsonian style.

William Robinson (1838–1935) was born in County Down and worked in various Irish gardens before having a row with his employer at Ballykilvan, County Laois, and storming out, leaving the hot houses open and unheated. He went to England, where he became a critic of the formal flower garden, advocating a more natural approach to planting. His aim was to create gardens that looked as if they had just 'happened' and were easy to maintain. He wrote a number of very influential books on his theories, including *The Wild Garden* and *The English Flower Garden*.

The Mount Usher Gardens originally covered not much more than an acre, but today extend to twenty acres and contain a collection of 5,000 of the finest varieties of trees and shrubs from across the world, assembled together here in a natural, romantic landscape. The presence of the River Vartry, which flows through the long, narrow site with frequent weirs, is of prime importance: it provides the most wonderful vistas, doubling the beauty of the foliage and flowers through its reflections, and producing a constant sibilant and restful sound. Frequent glimpses of the double-bow-fronted Mount Usher House add to the visual delight; not many photographers will escape with film left in their cameras. My favourite tree at Mount Usher is the glorious Montezuma pine, a native of Mexico that is like a burst of fireworks frozen in time.

Leaving Mount Usher, head north through Ashford village, cross the river by the Ashford House Bar and turn left at the roundabout. After a few hundred metres bear right at a Y-junction signed for Roundwood.

A short distance along here, on the left, are the gates to the extensive Ballycurry demesne. Ballycurry House is an eighteenth-century house that was rebuilt in 1808 to the designs of Francis Johnston. An early owner, Charles Tottenham, MP, was famous for riding 96km (60 miles) through the night and arriving mud-spattered to attend the first sitting in the new Parliament Building in Dublin (now the Bank of Ireland) to vote against surplus revenue being handed to the English government.

The house features in the film of Molly Keane's novel, *Time after Time*.

Soon the road swings around towards the west and climbs through a pretty valley to a craggy pass, beyond which the Wicklow Mountains line the horizon. The western side of the pass presents a very different landscape from that on the east, with gorse-decorated stone walls and few trees compared to the extravagant foliage and green pastures of the east side.

Less than 8.5km (5.3 miles) from Ashford, Vartry Reservoir at Roundwood appears ahead. The road bends sharply to the left and runs along the top of a causeway dam at the southern end of the reservoir. The River Vartry, which we previously saw overhung by exotic trees and shrubs in Mount Usher Gardens and, a little further upstream, flowing through Ashford, has here been interrupted in its 29km (18 miles) journey to the sea to provide a reservoir that supplies 80 million litres of water to Dublin, Dún Laoghaire, Bray and Wicklow town every day. The scheme was constructed between 1862 and 1868 as the first major effort to address the increasing needs of the expanding capital for clean drinking water. Paths that circumnavigate the reservoir provide a pleasant walk of about two hours along the wooded shore, from where a variety of water birds, including herons and great-crested grebes, can be observed.

Continue westwards and enter the village of Roundwood 2.5km (1.6 miles) from the reservoir. The main street is about 230m above sea-level, and locals boast that it is the highest village in Ireland. If you wish to delay your return to Dublin, there is a number of places here where you can take evening refreshments. *The Tourist's Handbook* of 1851 states that 'this secluded hamlet, embosomed in the midst of mountains' ... has 'two comfortable inns, whose charges are as moderate as their fare is excellent ...' The two inns still survive and thrive: the Roundwood Inn, where you will find a log fire alight well into the warm season, and opposite it, the Coach House.

Leaving Roundwood, take the R755 northwards up the valley of the upper Vartry to Calary and Ballyremon Commons, and soon after you will once more pass under the cone of the Great Sugar Loaf. The road swings around to the east and descends through the scenic Rocky Valley to reach the N11 at Kilmacanoge, where you turn left and return, via the M11, to the M50 and Dublin.

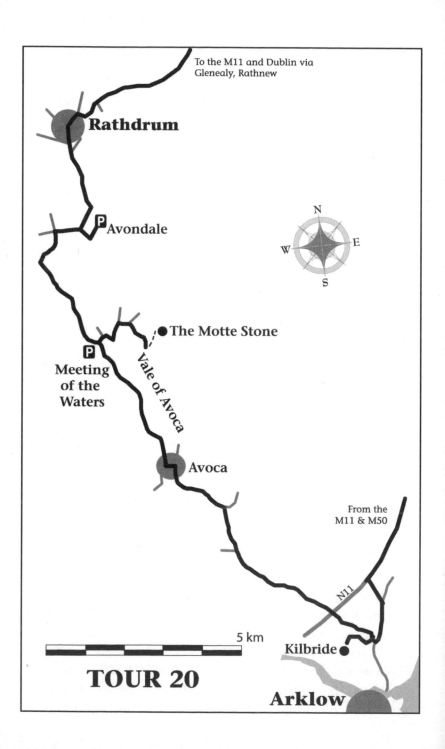

To the M11 and Dublin via
Glenealy, Rathnew

Rathdrum

P Avondale

N
W E
S

● The Motte Stone

P

Vale of Avoca

**Meeting
of the
Waters**

Avoca

From the
M11 & M50

N11

5 km

Kilbride ●

TOUR 20

Arklow

The Vale of Avoca and Avondale Forest Park, Co. Wicklow

ﬁ

Avondale, County Wicklow, is the birthplace of Charles Stewart Parnell (1846–1891), the 'uncrowned king of Ireland', and the house and demesne, now owned by Coillte, provide plenty to do and see for old and young alike. Interesting places along our route via the Vale of Avoca to Avondale include an unusual and mysterious mausoleum, the TV village of Ballykissangel, the Meeting of the Waters, made famous by Tom Moore's song, and the Motte Stone, a dramatic hilltop glacial erratic that has been attracting tourists for 200 years.

ROUTE: The M11 and N11 are followed almost as far south as Arklow, and then the route follows minor roads to Avoca, the Meeting of the Waters and on to Avondale, which is near the town of Rathdrum. The return to Dublin is via the R752 through Rathdrum and Rathnew to rejoin the M11.

DISTANCE: 112km (70 miles).

MAPS: OS Discovery numbers 50, 56 and 62.

The route starts at the south-eastern end of the M50, where it becomes the M11, and the journey south through County Wicklow is a scenic one, weaving past the Little Sugar Loaf with its twin summit and, soon after, the towering, conical, grey-streaked Great Sugar Loaf. South of Kilmacanoge is the wooded Glen of the Downs, and not long after comes a grand view of the humpy Wicklow Head extending out into the Irish Sea and topped by two lighthouses. Bypass Wicklow town, and after about 51km (32 miles) from the M50 turn left off the Arklow bypass onto a road signed 'Arklow'. When you reach the outskirts of the town, and just after crossing Ticknock Bridge, look out on the right for a road signed to Avoca, and turn onto it. After about 200m take a short detour down a narrow road to the left in order to visit one of the finest mausoleums on the east coast. Kilbride Churchyard is a little more than 0.8km (0.5 mile) down this road, on the left. A narrow, grass-covered laneway leads to the churchyard, which is dominated by the massive pyramidic mausoleum of the Howard family, described by Maurice Craig as 'one of the most romantic and mysterious of Irish mausolea'.

The monument is in two parts: the lower, Egyptian-columned entrance built into the side of the great mound that is the graveyard; and the pyramid, which projects out of the top of the mound from amidst a collection of interesting old tombstones. Looking for all the world like a set from *Raiders of the Lost Ark*, it was erected in 1785 by Ralph Howard, Viscount Wicklow, to the designs of Simon Vierpyl, an Italian brought to Ireland by Lord Charlemont. The Howards lived in nearby Shelton Abbey, which in 1819 was transformed into an opulent Gothic Revival masterpiece to the designs of Sir Richard Morrison. The Abbey was sold out of the family in 1951 and for some time it was a school, but for the last number of years has been an open prison; I'm sure Ralph is turning in his mausoleum! Sir John Parnell, grandfather of Charles Stewart Parnell, is also buried in this graveyard. Of the church of Kilbride, mentioned as being extant in 1216, only a few ivy-covered fragments remain.

Return to the road for Avoca and turn left. A very pleasant drive of under 8km (5 miles) takes you to the village of Avoca; on the way, off to the left, Crohan Kinsella Mountain fills the horizon. It was here in the late eighteenth century, in the Aughatinavough River, that large nuggets of gold were found, leading to a brief but frantic goldrush. It was harvest-time, but there was not a single farm labourer to be found to save the crops; they were all digging up the mountain. Local landowners had to petition the government to control the situation. The Army moved in and sent the amateur miners packing, but not before they had found a further 800 ounces of gold. Subsequently, and in spite of further extensive explorations conducted by expert geologists, little else was found. People still, however, more as a hobby, pan for gold in the streams coming off the mountain, sometimes with mild success. As the road reaches the brow of a hill and starts descending into the Avoca valley, there is a fine vista ahead of the southern foothills of the Wicklow Mountains.

The pretty village of Avoca became famous in the closing years of the twentieth century as the location for the television series, *Ballykissangel*, and it still receives coach-loads of visitors who are fans of the show and want to be photographed in front of well-known landmarks, such as the pub.

Prior to its recent television fame, Avoca was well-known for its weaving mills, and probably will be long after the TV fans have taken their last photograph. The Avoca Mill is a family-run company, founded some 280 years ago. Early in the company's history, in 1760, a revolutionary new machine was introduced to speed up the weaving process: the Fly Shuttle Loom could produce 20m of cloth a day. Some of these looms are still in use today in Avoca; after all this time they remain the fastest method of hand-weaving ever devised. In the 1920s Avoca Handweavers' tweeds were known all over the world, and even favoured by Parisian designers. In the 1950s Avoca tweed was used for a waistcoat for King George VI and to make baby blankets for Prince Charles and Princess Anne.

If you pause a while in Avoca, you can visit the mills (admission is free) and watch this famous tweed being made. There is a fine product shop, and a small café serving inexpensive snacks.

Leaving the village, cross the bridge and turn right onto the R752 and head north up along the Vale of Avoca. The vale is rich in minerals, particularly copper, which has been mined here, with frequent interruptions, since the Bronze Age. In recent centuries sulphur, iron and ochre have also been taken from the ground in commercial quantities, and lead, zinc, gold and silver are also present. Intensive copper-mining was begun in the mid-eighteenth century, and by the early 1800s as many as 1,000 people worked the mines here, with boys and men working underground, while women and girls sorted the crushed ore on the surface. At that time there were 140 vertical shafts in the mines and 50km of horizontal tunnels. Mining declined through the end of the nineteenth and beginning of the twentieth century, but there was a brief revival in the 1950s when 450 men were employed for a few years, during which thousands of tons of copper ore were shipped out of Arklow port. A drop in world copper prices in the early 1960s tolled the death-knell of copper-mining in the area, and mining activities finally ceased completely in 1982.

There is frequent evidence of former mining efforts visible along the valley. Widespread tree-planting has as yet failed to hide great spoil heaps of garish-coloured clays, chimneys, engine houses and the remains of the mine railway that connected Avoca to Arklow and was the first railway to be built in County Wicklow.

Just over 3km (2 miles) north of Avoca we reach the place where Avonbeg River joins with Avonmore River to become the Avoca, a scenic place called 'The Meeting of the Waters'. It was made famous in song all over the world by the poet Tom Moore, often called Ireland's National Poet, who was born in Dublin in 1779. In London, where he went to study law, he found that his poetical and musical talents opened many doors, and before long his music had become extraordinarily popular. At the height of his career Moore's popularity was such that he enjoyed a status equal to any top film actor or popstar of our day. It was on a visit to Wicklow in 1807 that he wrote the song that put Avoca on the map, which begins with the words:

There is not in this wide world a valley so sweet
As the vale in whose bosom the bright waters meet ...

If you want to stay a while here, you can park near the extensive public house and souvenir shop, The Meetings, which overlooks the 'meeting', serves good food and hosts an outdoor *ceili* on summer Sundays (tel: 0402 35226). Make your way down to the wheelchair-friendly little park from where 'The Meeting of the Waters' can be viewed. The old oak tree under which Moore wrote the song was venerated for many years, but is now reduced to a skeletal baulk.

Leave The Meeting of the Waters and continue north across the bridge. The Motte Stone, a well-known local landmark and viewpoint, is less than 2.5km (1.5 miles) away. If you want to visit it, take the first turn to the right after the bridge.

Follow the narrow road uphill and bear right at a Y-junction, crossing the Avoca River again over the Lion Arch bridge. The gates to Castle Howard are passed on the right as the road begins to climb between heather-covered hedges through pleasant beech and birch woodland. Turn right at a cottage, and a few hundred metres on, turn right again. Over 1km (0.6 mile) further on, when the tarmac road surface becomes gravel and the road begins to descend again, there is space to park the car at the verge.

The Motte Stone is a gentle fifteen- to twenty-minutes walk away from here, up the gravel track that veers sharply to the left. The track is hedged with gorse stitched with heather, fraochains and an occasional escapee rhododendron ponticum, and as it ascends the hillside great views unfold off to the left. Down in the sylvan valley Castle Howard comes into view, a romantic early nineteenth-century castle designed by Sir Richard Morrison; it was here that Tom Moore was staying as a guest when he wrote 'The Meeting of the Waters' in the summer of 1807. To the west Crohan Moira, the southern portal to Glenmalure and the beginning of the southern Wicklow range, can be seen. When the hedge to the right comes to an end you can cut across the heathered hillside, following a sheep track for 50m to reach a clay path. Turn right and follow it for about 70m to reach the Motte Stone at the summit of the hill.

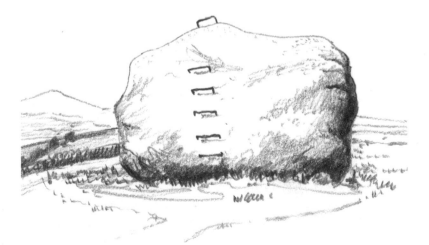

The Motte Stone

The Motte Stone became a minor tourist attraction in Victorian times, and many a fine picnic was enjoyed at its base. The great granite boulder, 12m in circumference, is an isolated glacial erratic, dropped here thousands of years ago by the retreating ice of the last Ice Age. In the 1880s iron ladder-rungs were fixed into the stone by a Captain Oates (I wonder was it he of the Antarctic?) to allow the rock to be easily climbed.

The views from the top of the stone are wonderful: the highest mountain in Leinster, Lugnaquillia, can be seen to the west, standing protectively over the deep valley of Glenmalure, while to the east the glistening Irish Sea fills the horizon, and to the north the tip of the cone of Great Sugar Loaf reaches over the tops of the intervening hills. Directly south is a huge, orange-coloured hill of spoil, a product of the most recent mining and which gives an indication of the massive amounts of material moved during the process. Beyond it, the craggy summit on the horizon is Crohan Kinsella, the goldrush mountain.

Returning to the car and to the R752, turn right. About 3.2km (2 miles) on take a turn right, signposted for Avondale, and take the next left to reach the gates of the estate. There are two admission charges to Avondale House: €5 for the car park, which gives access to all the estate grounds, and a further €5 per person if you want to visit the house, while a family ticket for the garden and the house can be had for €15. (For up-to-date information on opening hours and admission fees, tel: 0404 46111.)

Avondale House was built in 1777 by Samuel Hayes, barrister, MP and a founder member of the Botanical Gardens in Dublin. Hayes was an enthusiastic devotee of trees and forestry, and in 1794 wrote the first, and one of the finest, book on forestry written in Ireland. The Irish climate is ideal for silviculture, and up until the 1500s the country was thickly forested with great trees. Over the succeeding centuries, however, the country was denuded of trees in the cause of iron-smelting and timber export to Britain for building and shipping. When afforestation became popular among landowners in Britain in the late eighteenth century, some Irish landowners were similarly enthused, including Hayes. He set about putting new ideas of cultivation into practice at Avondale, and some of the trees he planted still prosper all these years later. The estate passed to the Parnell family in 1795. The Parnells established a sawmill, and continued to plant and harvest good timber until the estate had to be sold in 1894. The State acquired it in 1904 and began the establishment of an experimental forestry plantation, the work of which continues today.

The forest park is over 200 acres in extent, and offers a variety of waymarked walking trails for the visitor, details of which are outlined in a brochure available for €2.50.

The Exotic Tree Trail is about 2.3km (1.4 miles) long, and includes some steps. It takes you past eucalyptus trees from Australia, silver firs planted in the 1780s by Samuel Hayes and giant and spectacular sequoia trees, natives of California and representatives of the largest and oldest of all living organisms on Earth.

The Pine Trail is about 1.75km (just over 1 mile) long and takes you through a collection of deciduous and conifer trees, including Spanish chestnuts, yews, junipers, larches and rhododendrons.

The Cairn Walk is about 2.3km (1.4 miles) long and takes in elements of the previous two walks.

The River Walk is about 5.2km (3.25 miles) long; there are some steep ascents and descents and sturdy footwear is recommended. It takes you through the woodland and along the banks of the fast-flowing Avonmore River, where there are some spots with little beaches and stepping-stones that are safe for supervised children to play, or even paddle, and in summertime ideal for picnics.

In recent years Avondale House has been restored and established as a museum to the memory of Charles Stewart Parnell. The house is thought to have been designed by the English architect John Wyatt—the initials 'JW' are carved on the inside of the main door—and is entered through a fine, bright, two-storey hall decorated with Gothic plasterwork and overlooked by a gallery. Of particular note is the Wedgewood-blue dining room with neo-classical plasterwork on the walls and ceilings attributed to the Italian Francini brothers, who must have been kept busy for years in Ireland, and the bow room with its beautiful Bossi fireplace.

At the height of a brilliant political career, during which he frequently had the English Parliament tied up in knots, Charles Stewart

Parnell was on the verge of achieving Home Rule for Ireland when his work was ended by the scandal attending his affair with a married woman, Kitty O'Shea. Devastated by the reversal of public opinion against him, Parnell died in England at the early age of forty-five. His body was returned to Ireland and buried in Glasnevin Cemetery amidst emotional scenes of public mourning.

There are lots of fine picnic spots to enjoy at Avondale, and children will enjoy the commando training-type playground, constructed from logs with ropes, etc. There is also a café and gift shop in the basement of the house, and toilet facilities.

To return to Dublin, take the R752 through Rathdrum and Glenealy to Rathnew, where the N11 and the outgoing route are rejoined.

SELECT BIBLIOGRAPHY

Casey, Christine and Alistair Rowan, *The Buildings of Ireland: North Leinster* (Penguin, London, 1993)

Costello, Con, *Guide to Kildare and West Wicklow* (Leinster Leader, Naas, 1991)

Costello, Con, *Looking Back: Aspects of History: County Kildare* (Leinster Leader, Naas, 1988)

Craig, Maurice, *The Architecture of Ireland from earliest times to 1880* (Batsford, London, 1982)

Craig, Maurice and Michael, *Mausolea Hibernica* (Lilliput, Dublin, 1999)

De Breffny, Brian and George Mott, *Churches and Abbeys of Ireland* (Thames and Hudson, London, 1976)

Fewer, Michael, *Irish Waterside Walks* (Gill & Macmillan, Dublin, 1997)

Fewer, Michael, *Walking Across Ireland: From Dublin Bay to Galway Bay* (The Collins Press, Cork, 2003)

Foster, John Wilson and Helena C.G. Chesney (eds.), *Nature in Ireland: A Scientific and Cultural History* (Lilliput, Dublin, 1997)

Healy, Patrick, *Archaeology, Early Christian Remains and Local Histories: Paddy Healy's Dublin* (South Dublin Libraries, Dublin, 2003)

Herity, Michael, *Irish Passage Graves: Neolithic tomb-builders in Ireland and Britain 2500 B.C.* (Irish U.P., Dublin, 1974)

Heron, Marianne, *The Hidden Gardens of Ireland: where to find them* (Gill & Macmillan, Dublin, 1993)

Heron, Marianne, *The Hidden Houses of Ireland: where to find them* (Gill & Macmillan, Dublin, 1999)

Howley, James, *The Follies and Garden Buildings of Ireland* (Yale University Press, London, 2003)

Jones, Mark Bence, *A Guide to Irish Country Houses* (Constable, London, 1988)

Killanin, Lord, Michael Duignan & Peter Harbison, *The Shell Guide to Ireland* (Gill & Macmillan, Dublin, 1995)

Lewis, Samuel, *A Topographical Dictionary of Ireland* (John Goulding, Wexford, 2000)

McMann, Jean, *Loughcrew: The Cairns* (After Hours Books, Oldcastle, 1993)

Moriarty, Christopher, *On Dublin's Doorstep: exploring the province of Leinster* (Wolfhound Press, Dublin, 2002)

Mulvihill, Mary, *Ingenious Ireland: a county-by-county exploration of Irish mysteries and marvels* (TownHouse & CountryHouse, Dublin, 2002)

Newby, Eric and Diana Petry, *Wonders of Ireland and how to find them* (Hodder & Stoughton, London, 1969)

O'Donnell, Ruan, *Exploring Wicklow's Rebel Past: 1798–1803* (Wicklow '98 Committee, Wicklow, 1999)

O'Farrell, Padraic, *The Book of Mullingar* (Uisneach Press, Mullingar, 1986)

O'Maitiu, Seamus and Barry O'Reilly, *Ballyknockan: a Wicklow stonecutters' village* (Woodfield Press, Dublin, 1997)

Simms, Anngret and J.H. Andrews (eds.), *More Irish Country Towns* (Mercier Press in association with RTÉ, Dublin, 1995)